love

LOVE DIGS DEEP

Cheryl L. Black

Belleville, Ontario, Canada

Love Digs Deep

Library and Archives Canada Cataloguing in Publication

Black, Cheryl L. (Cheryl Ladell), 1948-

Love digs deep / Cheryl L. Black.

Includes bibliographical references.

ISBN 1-55452-043-6

1. Spiritual formation. 2. Soils--Religions aspects--Christianity.

I. Title.

BV4501.3.B525 2006   248.4   C2006-901351-9

You may contact Evangelist Cheryl Black for book orders or speaking appointments at:

VOH, LLC
PMB 193, 14311 Newport Ave, #G
Tustin, CA 92780-5662
www.vohllc.com

Guardian Books is an imprint of *Essence Publishing,* a Christian Book Publisher dedicated to furthering the work of Christ through the written word.. For more information, contact:

20 Hanna Court, Belleville, Ontario, Canada K8P 5J2
Phone: 1-800-238-6376 • Fax: (613) 962-3055
E-mail: publishing@essencegroup.com • Internet: www.essencegroup.com

Dedication

This book is dedicated to both of my pastors: Pastor Clemmon T. Anderson of Greater Rose of Sharon Church of God in Christ in Detroit, Michigan; and Bishop Noel Jones of City of Refuge in Gardena, California. I truly thank God for both of you and the ministries He has placed within you. He gave both of you such great anointing and rich deposits of His truths. Thank you both for giving and giving and giving and giving! Thank you both for preaching and teaching and teaching and preaching! Thank you both for not lowering the standard of holiness but keeping it lifted high, so that I had to continually strive to come up. And thank you both for the love you have given me.

And we beseech you, brethren, to know them which labor among you, and are over you in the Lord, and admonish you; and to esteem them very highly in love for their work's sake (1 Thessalonians 5:12-13a).

My Prayer

Father, in the name of Jesus, bless this book, I pray, and help us to break up the fallow ground in our lives. Stir the hearts and minds of Your people everywhere. Open up the blinded eyes and unstop the deaf ears. Take away the division, and bring about the love and unity that You intended us to have, in Jesus name. Amen!

Table of Contents

Acknowledgement

To my friend, Florence Felton: thank you for your love and willingness to share your knowledge and skills in this endeavor. Thank you for your attentiveness to details, whenever I expressed my thoughts to you, because it is truly reflected in the cover. I could not have done it without you. May God reward you, abundantly, for your kindness.

Foreword

Sister Cheryl, you are a living testimony to the fact that God is still on the throne, sitting high and looking low, affecting the affairs of mankind. As yielded vessels to His transforming power, He works in us, out of us and through us those things that may be most beneficial to us and to others. As a source of encouragement to others, you, through the means of inspirational, apologetic writing, defending your hope in Christ and trust in God have gone on record to strengthen the faithful and inform the doubters that God is faithful to His Word, that He is "*able to do exceeding abundantly above all that we ask or think, by the power that worketh in us*" (Ephesians 3:20).

As the readers of this book view the record of your personal walk through the dark valleys of trouble, trial and sacrifice, tears and pain, they may be able to derive comfort in knowing that God is, indeed and in fact, the God of all comfort in any undesirable circumstance, as recorded in 2 Corinthians. Just as He has been your source of unfailing peace and comfort in the midst of the storms of life, He can be relied upon and trusted to do likewise for others who place their confidence in Him. 2 Corinthians 1:3-4 states,

> *Blessed be God, even the Father of our Lord Jesus Christ, the Father of mercies, and the God of all comfort; Who comforteth us in all our tribulation, that we may be able to comfort them which are in*

> *any trouble, by the comfort wherewith we ourselves are comforted of God.*

It is true, love does dig deep; it is also true that God is the greatest source of love, indeed, the very epitome of love. He defines, describes and manifests love to us, as recorded in 1 John 4:8b-11,

> *For God is love. In this was manifested the love of God toward us, because that God sent his only begotten Son into the world, that we might live through him. Herein is love, not that we loved God, but that he loved us, and sent his Son to be the propitiation for our sins. Beloved, if God so loved us, we ought also to love one another.*

May God bless all who are blessed through the writing and reading of *Love Digs Deep*!

PASTOR CLEMMON T. ANDERSON
Greater Rose of Sharon C.O.G.I.C.

Preface

Jesus taught the people using the following parable:

> *A sower went out to sow his seed: and as he sowed, some fell by the way side; and it was trodden down, and the fowls of the air devoured it. And some fell upon a rock; and as soon as it was sprung up, it withered away, because it lacked moisture. And some fell among thorns; and the thorns sprang up with it, and choked it. And other fell on good ground, and sprang up, and bare fruit an hundredfold. And when he had said these things, he cried, He that hath ears to hear, let him hear* (St. Luke 8:5-8).

The question is, what is your soil type? If you are not producing fruit, why not ask the Lord to clear away the rocks and thorns in your life, so that you can produce? The prophet Jeremiah exhorted the house of Judah saying,

> *For thus saith the LORD to the men of Judah and Jerusalem, Break up your fallow ground, and sow not among thorns* (Jeremiah 4:3).

Fallow simply means uncultivated, barren, crop-free, unproductive and uncreative. You have to take the initiative to cultivate your spirit, by not only going to church to have the word preached to you; but, you have to get involved by fasting and praying and asking the Lord to show you yourself and, take out of you those things that prohibit you from producing. Cultivating your soil, also, means you have to study and search out those things which you claim to have a hope in.

Through the years of my life, I have had to check my own soil to see who or what I was. Because at different stages and times in my life, I found myself to be one or another of the various soil types that Jesus mentioned in His parable. But, after much breaking by and fertilization of the word of God I have, finally, begun to bare fruit. And it has taken a long time to get to the place where the Lord wanted me to be. So I am very appreciative of His love for me and longsuffering with me, until I keep striving. I keep trying to make something of this gift of life that He has given me.

> "*But grow in grace, and in the knowledge of our Lord and Savior Jesus Christ. To him be glory both now and for ever. Amen*" (II Peter 3:18).

CHAPTER 1

Apologetics from the Pew

Well, here He goes again! The Spirit of the Lord is pushing me again. I cannot say I do not know why or I do not understand, because He has already told me He has to redeem the time. It is so amazing to me how God matures us. He can bring you to a point where He does not want to hear any whining or complaining. He definitely is not accepting any excuses. He says to me, "I have delivered you, I have nurtured you, I have sustained you and I have provided for you. I have worked in your spirit and in your mind and showed you how to do what it is that I want you to do, so do it." And once again, I feel that sense of urgency.

Since my youthful years were spent supporting, encouraging and preparing my five children for life, I did not enter into the halls of the universities. But God did not preclude me from being an intelligent human being or being called into His service. I had wondered in my mind how the Lord was going to close out this series of writings He had put in me, especially since He had caused me to be so open about my life. But because this is the Lord's doing and He is in charge, He has made this a book of apologetics. Hopefully, through my references, I can make my position clear enough, so that future generations of Christians will understand that they too will have to take a stand for what they believe. A close friend and some of my family members have implied that my second book, *A Shepherd's Heart*, is controversial. However, for me, the significance of the book was that it was a modern-day testimony of God's power, mercy and grace. He has allowed me to live, and what He has taught me through every experience in my life has brought me to this point of sharing with you. However, I did realize it would stir up some controversy and opposition of some sort. Consequently, because there are those who question my motives and loyalty to my upbringing, it presents the opportunity for me to do something else I never thought I would be able to do. So, here is my endeavor on apologetics, which is not an apology by any means. The Lord has given me to write this book in defense of the gospel on which I stand and I feel very privileged and grateful. Now I have got to draw on everything the Lord has put in me, and I pray it will help someone.

Some call it name-dropping, but I call it giving honor and credit where honor and credit is due. I have not lived my life in a vacuum; I live in a society with people. And people in one way or another have influenced my life, whether positively or negatively. Also, I live in a significant and important time in history, because it seems as though many people have lost their determination and strength of mind to become all that God intended for them to be. They have allowed their circumstances and the environment in which we live to dictate their future; many have succumbed to mediocrity and given up on their dreams and aspirations. Born in 1948, after World War II, in the city of Detroit, I am a part of the baby-boomer generation that should have produced many more success stories than any other generation in history, because we were given the opportunities that many of our parents and grandparents did not have. But instead, it seems that so many are going down without a fight, and I'm just trying, in some way, to fan the flames of hope.

I Was Taught

I grew up in the North on the east side of Detroit. Although I am Black, I went to elementary school with children from other ethnic backgrounds, such as Italians, Poles, Germans and even two young Chinese boys. I grew up in a Christian home, and because I did not grow up in a segregated community, I did not experience many of the prejudices that many of my brothers and sisters in the South experienced, until the sixties and seventies. When I was in middle school, I had nuns from the Catholic church as teachers. And when school was out for the summer, we went to the Episcopalian church around the corner from our house for our summer activities. I was taught the Bible early in my life. And the golden rule was to do unto others, as you would have them do unto you.

> *Therefore all things whatsoever ye would that men should do to you, do ye even so to them: for this is the law and the prophets* (Matthew 7:12).

Civil unrest in the South intensified and exploded on the scene during my high-school years, and then I became increasingly aware of the prejudices of others around me because of the White flight to the suburbs. As I grew up, I was taught about the judgment and love of God. But unfortunately, I was not taught about the hatred and cruelty of people. I was taught not to hate anyone; I was taught to love people. I was taught not to fight; I was taught to turn the other cheek and to run from the fight. I was not taught to stand my ground, and because I was always being told to shut up and hush, I was taught that my opinions were not important.

Since my grandfather was a pastor, we went to church not just on Sundays but also every Tuesday and Friday night. I was taught to fast on service nights, even as a child. Although he did not attend seminary, my grandfather studied and knew the word of God. God revealed Himself to him, and he was anointed. He had an understanding of the word that was pronounced, and he would argue the scriptures with the best of his friends in the barber shop. God gave him faith to believe Him. And he taught us in his own simple way that if God said "go through that wall," you just start moving in that direction, believing Him to make a way before you get there. He was a preacher, and he was a provider for his family. He instructed me not to look at other people's actions in the church, because they may cause you to stumble in your walk with God. You have to keep your eyes on the Lord. He instructed me not to open my heart to everything. When he passed away, the mantle was passed to my uncle, Pastor Clemmon Anderson, who labored with me and nurtured me in the way of the Lord for over thirty-four years.

Some preachers and teachers today feel like it is necessary to criticize and tear up everything from the past. They seem determined to tear up any remnants of past traditions, instead of building upon the foundation that has already been laid. That is astonishing to me, since God said there is nothing new under the sun. Although I do agree that some traditions need to be discarded, I believe we should first take a serious, objective look at what is ineffective and then decide what we need to hold onto.

Paul said,

> *Now he that planteth and he that watereth are one: and every man shall receive his own reward according to his own labour. For we are labourers together with God: ye are God's husbandry, ye are God's building. According to the grace of God which is given unto me, as a wise master builder, I have laid the foundation, and another buildeth thereon. But let every man take heed how he buildeth thereupon. For other foundation can no man lay than that is laid, which is Jesus Christ* (1 Corinthians 3:8-11).

Yes, this is a new millennium. Yes, times have changed, and a whole lot of things have changed with the times. And yes, God has given deeper revelations of His truths. But when I hear the same opinions, attitudes and judgments concerning denominational separation that were expressed during my grandfather's lifetime, I am saddened and dismayed, because there are many souls who still need to be won and there are more critical issues that need to be dealt with within the body of the church. And it seems to be extremely hard to get people to a place of unity of spirit and love. And that is another reason why it is difficult to get this country back to a place of genuine faith in God, because the emphasis in the church has shifted so far to the left. Everyone who believes and preaches that Jesus Christ is the Son of God, and that He died on the cross, was buried, rose again from the dead and sent the Holy Ghost to give us power and to lead us and guide us into all truths then, surely, we ought to have unity because Christ only has one body, one bride—the Church. And for all of us who profess to be Christian, we are a part of that same body. And for those who have not matured enough in the word of God, I can only pray that God will give you understanding. Jesus said,

> *Search the scriptures; for in them ye think ye have eternal life: and they are they which testify of me* (St. John 5:39).

Here is another conversation that Jesus had with his disciples:

> *And John answered him, saying, Master, we saw one casting out devils in thy name, and he followeth not us: and we forbad him, because he followeth not us. But Jesus said, forbid him not: for there is no man which shall do a miracle in my name, that can lightly speak evil of me. For he that is not against us is on our part* (St. Mark 9:38-40).

When the Lord directed me to the City of Refuge in April 2002, I held a current Church of God in Christ National Evangelist license that did not expire until September, 2003. I had already gone through the learning and training of church protocol. I had been a Sunday-school teacher and the superintendent in my local church. I had been a district worker working with children and young people, and I also had been a jurisdictional or state worker in the Great Lakes Ecclesiastical Jurisdiction of Michigan, under the leadership of the late Bishop Cleveland L. Anderson, Jr. and Mother Merle R. Cranford, as co-president of the Young Women's Christian Council. I was taught to be submissive to leadership. I was taught that in order to be a good leader, you must first be a good follower. My knowledge of and involvement in church work has been extensive.

Going to New Levels

But the Holy Spirit led me to an apostolic church, and licenses or credentials are not transferable from one denomination to another. However, that did not negate the call of God on my life. And Paul told us,

> *I therefore, the prisoner of the Lord, beseech you that ye walk worthy of the vocation wherewith ye are called, With all lowliness and meekness, with longsuffering, forbearing one another in love; Endeavouring to keep the unity of the Spirit in the bond of peace. There is one body, and one Spirit, even as ye are called in one hope of your calling; One Lord, one faith, one baptism, One God and Father of all, who is above all, and through all, and in you all* (Ephesians 4:1-6).

I did not know the pastor or the church affiliation when I joined. The young lady who brought me to the church moved to Oakland but the Lord did not tell me to move. In fact, He renewed my strength, He refreshed my spirit, He sustained me. He restored the joy of my salvation, even in the midst of my hardest trial. At that time, I was crying a lot for two reasons: first, because my youngest son was in jail in Oklahoma; and second, because the Lord was pulling me completely out of my comfort zone. And all I had to hold onto was His word. So I could not look at the pastor or the church affiliation. All I knew about this man, Bishop Noel Jones, was that he was preaching the truth of the gospel. Hebrews 4:12 says,

For the word of God is quick, and powerful, and sharper than any twoedged sword, piercing even to the dividing asunder of soul and spirit, and of the joints and marrow, and is a discerner of the thoughts and intents of the heart.

And I needed every word that God would send me. I knew nothing was hid from the Lord, but I had no idea that He was going to open me up for the world to see.

Neither is there any creature that is not manifest in his sight: but all things are naked and opened unto the eyes of him with whom we have to do (Hebrews 4:13).

But who are these people who we call preachers of the gospel, and what is it that they preach? Personally, why have I given them such a significant and special place in my life? The answer is simple. They are fishers of men; they are God's ambassadors, and they preach the good news of Jesus Christ! And the reason they have such a special place in my heart is because without the preaching of the word of God, I would be eternally, lost. If I had not heard the message of hope and deliverance that they preached, I would still be living my life void of understanding and peace. The Prophet Isaiah said,

Who hath believed our report? and to whom is the arm of the LORD *revealed?* (Isaiah 53:1)

And the Apostle Paul said,

For whosoever shall call upon the name of the Lord shall be saved. How then shall they call on him in whom they have not believed? and how shall they believe on him of whom they have not heard? and

how shall they hear without a preacher? And how shall they preach, except they be sent? as it is written, How beautiful are the feet of them that preach the gospel of peace, and bring glad tidings of good things (Romans 10:13-15).

The Lord called me to be an evangelist, which means that I must walk in my calling. And not only has He proven to me that He called me, but He has taught me that He can use me in whatever manner He chooses to get the job done. I do not have to be standing in a pulpit to preach or teach in order to spread the good news. And I do not have to hold a denominational license to do what He has called me to do. I need simply to listen for His voice and follow the leading of the Holy Spirit. Paul said,

And he gave some apostles; and some, prophets; and some, evangelists; and some, pastors and teachers; For the perfecting of the saints, for the work of the ministry, for the edifying of the body of Christ: Till we all come in the unity of the faith, and of the knowledge of the Son of God, unto a perfect man, unto the measure of the stature of the fulness of Christ (Ephesians 4:11-13).

We talk about going to new levels, but what does that really mean, if we do not exercise ourselves in or make use of the things that we are being taught? Paul admonished Timothy,

But watch thou in all things, endure afflictions, do the work of an evangelist, make full proof of thy ministry (2 Timothy 4:5).

When Bishop Jones preaches, because he is an intellectual, most times he is quoting somebody to embellish the text. And this stirred my mind as well as my spirit, until I had to search out the validity of what he was saying. God gave me a pastor who pours out his heart, mind and soul into His people, and somehow He connected my spirit to his. The Lord was using him to funnel all the knowledge He had allowed him to acquire into me. No, I did not get the college degree that I wanted, but God gave me a pastor to feed me with knowledge and understanding. And isn't that the word of God?

> *And I will give you pastors according to mine heart, which shall feed you with knowledge and understanding* (Jeremiah 3:15).

The Bondage of the Will

Consequently, I cannot just sit under this great outpouring of God's word and do nothing. What excuse would I give to the Lord at the judgment?

So now I quote from Martin Luther's *The Bondage of the Will*,[1] in defense of my crossing denominational boundaries. Luther says,

> "When the Word of God comes, it comes to change and renew the world; and even heathen writers acknowledge that such changes cannot take place without commotion and upheaval, nor, indeed, without bloodshed."

He also stated,

> "This is our contention: that spirits must be detected and tried by a double judgment. The first is internal. By it, through the enlightening of the Holy Ghost, the special gift of God, one enjoys complete certainty in judging of and deciding between the doctrines and opinions of all

> men as they affect oneself and one's own personal salvation. Of this judgment it is said in 1 Corinthians: 'The spiritual man judges all things, but he himself is judged by no man' (1 Corinthians 2:15) It belongs to faith, and is needful for every Christian, even for a layman.
>
> "The second is an external judgment. By it, we judge the spirits and doctrines of all men, also with the greatest certainty, and not now for ourselves only, but also for the benefit and salvation of others. This judgment is the province of the public ministry of the Word and the external office and is the special concern of teachers and preachers of the Word. We employ it when we strengthen the weak in faith and refute opponents."

So even as a layperson, I have a responsibility to make use of the things that I am being taught. And the Holy Ghost helps me in my judgments concerning the doctrines of men. Paul put it this way,

> *Let your speech be alway with grace, seasoned with salt, that ye may know how ye ought to answer every man* (Colossians 4:6).

And Peter put it another way,

> *But sanctify the Lord God in your hearts: and be ready always to give an answer to every man that asketh you a reason of the hope that is in you with meekness and fear: Having a good conscience; that, whereas they speak evil of you, as of evildoers, they may be ashamed that falsely accuse your good conversation in Christ* (1 Peter 3:15-16).

Almost every Sunday night when I was growing up, I attended Y.P.W.W., which stands for Young Peoples' Willing Workers. The study session was opened with the recitation of "Our Endeavor." This was written by the late Bishop O.T. Jones, Sr. and expanded upon by his son, Bishop O.T. Jones, Jr. The essence of that statement, for me, is that we must endeavor to have unity and harmony with those of like faith, we must develop spiritual fortitude, we must become servants and be willing to serve others and our thoughts should be invigorated from being taught and through our study of the scriptures, as we make every effort to live in the manner that God has ordained. My point is that was the emphasis of the "Our Endeavor" statement and I am still walking according to it, even though the Lord has united me to another church affiliation. I have not joined a cult. I am a Christian, and my hope is in Jesus Christ the Son of God, and I am standing on His word. I have experienced and gone through some horrific trials in my life, but God has sustained me. He has kept me alive, and He has kept my mind. All of my faith and confidence is in Him, and it has not been misplaced.

Dynamics of Faith

Also, I want to reference another great protestant philosopher and theologian of the twentieth century, whose writings Bishop Jones has introduced to me, and that is Paul Tillich. In his book *Dynamics of Faith*,[2] Paul Tillich says,

> "Faith is the state of being ultimately concerned: the dynamics of faith are the dynamics of man's ultimate concern. Man, like every living being, is concerned about many things, above all, about those which condition his very existence, such as food and shelter. But man, in contrast to other living beings, has spiritual concerns—cognitive, aesthetic, social and political. Some of them are

urgent, often extremely urgent, and each of them as well as the vital concerns can claim ultimacy for a human life or the life of a social group. If it claims ultimacy, it demands the total surrender of him who accepts this claim, and it promises total fulfillment even if all other claims have to be subjected to it or rejected in its name. Faith, for the men of the Old Testament, is the state of being ultimately and unconditionally concerned about Yahweh and about what He represents in demand threat and promise.

"Faith as ultimate concern is an act of the total personality. It happens in the center of the personal life and includes all its elements. Faith is the most centered act of the human mind. It is not a movement of a special section or a special function of man's total being. They are all united in the act of faith. Since faith is an act of the personality as a whole, it participates in the dynamics of personal life. Thinking in polarities, their tensions and their possible conflicts is a common characteristic of most of them. Man is able to decide for or against reason, he is able to create beyond reason or destroy below reason. This power is the power of his self, the center of self-relatedness in which all elements of his being are united. Faith is not an act of any of his rational functions, as it is not an act of the unconscious, but it is an act in which both the rational and the non-rational elements of his being are transcended.

"Faith as the embracing and centered act of the personality is 'ecstatic.' It transcends both the drives of the non-rational unconscious and the structures of the rational conscious. It transcends them, but it does not destroy them. In the ecstasy of faith, there is an awareness of truth and of ethical value; there are also past loves and hates, conflicts and reunions, individual and collective influences. 'Ecstasy' means 'standing outside of oneself'—without ceasing to be oneself—with all the elements which are united in the personal center. A further polarity in these elements, relevant for the understanding of faith, is the tension between the cognitive function of man's personal life, on the one hand and the emotion and will, on the other hand.

"There is certainly affirmation by the will of what concerns one ultimately, but faith is not a creation of the will. In the ecstasy of faith, the will to accept and to surrender is an element, but not the cause. And this is true also of feeling. Faith is not an emotional outburst; this is not the meaning of ecstasy. Certainly, emotion is in it, as in every act of man's spiritual life. But emotion does not produce faith. Faith has a cognitive content and is an act of the will.

"The reality of man's ultimate concern reveals something about his being, namely, that he is able to transcend the flux of relative and transitory experiences of his ordinary life. Man's experiences, feelings, thoughts are conditioned and finite. They not only come and go, but their content is of finite and conditional concern, unless they are elevated to unconditional validity. Human potentialities are powers that drive toward actualization. Man is driven toward faith by his awareness of the infinite to which he belongs, but which he does not own like a possession. This is in abstract terms what concretely appears as the 'restlessness of the heart' within the flux of life. The unconditional concern which is faith is the concern about the unconditional. The infinite passion, as faith has been described, is the passion for the infinite. Or, to use our first term, the ultimate concern is concern about what is experienced as ultimate."

All of that reads and sounds wonderful to me! And I truly hope you understood it and that you see my point. Because it is in reading and studying and listening and searching out what is being preached that you grow spiritually. It has certainly taken me to another level of intensity, and that is what this relationship with God is all about. But as good as it sounds, let me write it another way, so you'll understand me. My relationship and walk with God is my ultimate concern. So it does not matter whatever else I study or whatever else I may hear, it has to be proven by the word of God.

The theologians, philosophers and scholars lead us into deep waters. They stimulate our minds and our spirits to go searching for the riches of the word of God, and it is wonderful. Jesus said in His sermon on the mount,

> *Blessed are they which do hunger and thirst after righteousness: for they shall be filled* (Matthew 5:6).

He also told His disciples to launch out into the deep. For some reason, we tend to stay on the shore or close to the banks. We're afraid, for fear of failure, to venture out into the deep things of God. However, I told my children when I left Detroit, if I fail trying to do what the Lord has told me, at least I would have tried. James put it this way:

> *Even so faith, if it hath not works, is dead, being alone. Yea, a man may say, Thou hast faith, and I have works: shew me thy faith without thy works, and I will shew thee my faith by my works* (James 2:17-18).

I Was Led By the Spirit

Although I will not belabor the argument over which scripture is right or wrong, I must address it, since it is another issue of contention that was brought to my attention. I have been baptized using Matthew 28:19,

> *Go ye therefore, and teach all nations, baptizing them in the name of the Father, and of the Son, and of the Holy Ghost,*

because that is how my grandfather and Pastor Anderson baptized me. And I do not believe it was wrong. But I also have been baptized using the scripture, Acts 2:38,

> *Then Peter said unto them, Repent, and be baptized every one of you in the name of Jesus Christ for the remission of sins, and ye shall receive the gift of the Holy Ghost,*

because I was led by the Spirit to do so, and because this is the ordinance of the church of which I am now a member. And I surely do not believe the Holy Ghost would lead me to do anything wrong. And because the Lord cares and did not want me to have any conflict in my spirit, He comforted me through the words of Paul:

> *For though I be free from all men, yet have I made myself servant unto all, that I might gain the more* (1 Corinthians 9:19).

Also he said,

> *For as many as are led by the Spirit of God, they are the sons of God* (Romans 8:14).

And with that, I leave all the arguing to those who know more than me, and I will only say because of the simplicity of the gospel that I have received, they are both scriptural. So to all those who are in the academics of interpretation, you can go for it, because I am going to enjoy Jesus and this abundant life that He has led me into.

When we get stuck in our comfort zones, we tend to close our hearts and minds to new experiences that would lead us into the abundant life that is being preached. And I know I sound crazy to some of my family and friends when I tell them I believe God for certain things that He has put in my spirit. But the bottom line is, look at what He has done in me and through me. The difference is so enormous between my past and my present, and I am having a wonderful time. I tell you, the Lord tickles me and has me laughing at myself, simply because He will put something in my spirit, then He tells me I can do it. When I respond with all of my questions about how am I supposed to do it, He works it out in my mind, and I just put forth the effort. So I praise Him; I magnify Him; I give Him all the glory and honor because faith comes by hearing the word of God.

> *So then faith cometh by hearing, and hearing by the word of God* (Romans 10:17).

And believe me when I say I have done nothing in and of myself; it is all because of God's grace. Even faith is a gift of God, so I do not take any credit for what He is doing in and through me. Again Paul teaches us,

> *Now there are diversities of gifts, but the same Spirit. And there are differences of administrations, but the same Lord. And there are diversities of operations, but it is the same God which worketh all in all. But the manifestation of the Spirit is given to every man to profit withal. For to one is given by the Spirit the word of wisdom; to another the word of knowledge by the same Spirit; To another faith by the same Spirit; to another the gifts of healing by the same Spirit* (1 Corinthians 12:4-9).

And all gifts are given for the edifying of the body of Christ. My endeavor is to encourage and to help build up your faith in God.

Pastor Anderson brought me as far as he was supposed to, because there must always be a time of preparation, as it relates to the work of the Lord. And the Lord has shown me that in order for Him to take me to the next level of maturity, naturally and spiritually, He had to send me across the country and transplant me in another part of His vineyard, for which I am eternally grateful. When Jacob was dying, and he was praying for his sons, he said,

> *Joseph is a fruitful bough, even a fruitful bough by a well; whose branches run over the wall: The archers have sorely grieved him, and shot at him, and hated him: but his bow abode in strength, and the arms of his hands were made strong by the hands of the mighty God of Jacob; (from thence is the shepherd, the stone of Israel:)* (Genesis 49:22-24).

I was taught to look at the Old Testament to see how God dealt with His chosen people, and I could see how He would deal with me. And He has been faithful!

Chapter 2

Challenges to the Call

I reflect on the time of my calling, whenever I hear someone say they have always wanted to be a preacher or an evangelist, because I did not want to be either. I knew being called of God was no game. It is serious business speaking into the lives of other people. It is enough for me to be responsible and accountable for my own actions, and added to that was the responsibility for raising my children. So I did not want the additional responsibility for anyone else. Although I can teach and preach, I have no problem encouraging others in the work. Because personally, I wrestled with the Lord for a long time about calling me to something that I did not want to do. I never felt the need to be up front or on stage, so I thought to myself, let those persons do it who want to. Because some people strive to be in the limelight; they thrive on it! They enjoy it!

I accepted Jesus as Lord and Savior of my life in 1976. But I did not accept His call to the ministry until 1987, regardless of what other people said the Lord told them or what potential they saw in me, because I knew the call to ministry was sacred, and it meant more work and more responsibility. I knew it called for sacrifices, and the sacrifices could be great, and God calls us to the highest level of sacrifice, which is self-sacrifice. Because giving of oneself is what He requires. I had counted up that cost early in my life. I had seen the sacrifices of so many of the mothers in the church. I saw their labor. And as I got older, I felt and understood their pain. So no, I was not stepping up to the plate quickly. When I did accept the call of God on my life, I remember talking with Pastor Anderson. And finally, I felt like I was ready to go before the board of examiners for my missionary license. We talked about it, and then he asked me to wait another year to be sure, because I was single and he did not want me to make a shipwreck of the ministry. So he withheld his recommendation, and I waited to see if the Lord was going to relieve me of the burden He had put in my spirit. Since the Lord did not take the burden away, I went before the board and received C.O.G.I.C. licensing in 1988.

And as Jesus taught the multitude, He said,

> *For which of you, intending to build a tower, sitteth not down first, and counteth the cost, whether he have sufficient to finish it? Lest haply, after he hath laid the foundation, and is not able to finish it, all that behold it begin to mock him, Saying, this man began to build, and was not able to finish* (St. Luke 14:28-30).

I surrendered and submitted to His will, because the whipping from the consequences of my own behavior had been so crushing until "Yes, Lord" was my only saving grace. The trials and cares of my life had me crying out to Him constantly. So "Yes, Lord" became my answer. To this day, "Yes, Lord" is my response to His will. And I thank Him because it is not as difficult a struggle now, although it is still challenging. Nevertheless, I have learned and I understand that it is a privilege for me to be able to help someone else, especially because of all He has done for me. And I have experienced the joy of participating in someone else's spiritual growth, and that is a real blessing. It's like sprinkling a little water on a withered plant and in a couple of days seeing it revived. He may put something in my spirit to do that totally overwhelms me, but as long as He leads and guides me into it, I will go. And I will endeavor to do whatever He assigns to my hands to do because He is my life. Without Him I am nothing, and I can never repay Him. So I say like the Psalmist,

> *What shall I render unto the* LORD *for all his benefits toward me? I will take the cup of salvation, and call upon the name of the* LORD. *I will pay my vows unto the* LORD *now in the presence of all his people* (Psalm 116:12-14).

The Lord has done some tremendous things for me. He has brought me through some horrendous situations, and He wanted me to share the testimony of His goodness. He wanted me to encourage some people to stay in the race, because it is not easy to give out of yourself time and again, especially when those you give to do not have the ability to give back to you what it is you need, and it can become a struggle.

Prepared for New Challenges

When God calls you for a specific purpose, He prepares you in ways that are surprising. He had put in me the ability to nurture and foster hope in my five children, and He had put in me love and a sense of responsibility strong enough to hold onto my children no matter the challenges. What He had really done was prepare me for His service. And that was something I learned from one of my managers at a previous job. She wanted to promote me to foreclosure supervisor, and I did not want it. She asked me, "Why not?" I told her that I was already raising five children with different personalities and that was difficult enough. I did not want to be dealing with that at work too. She insisted that was the reason why she knew I could handle the job, not to mention the fact that I had the technical knowledge to train everyone who came through the door. So that is what God does: He saves you to serve and He prepares you for the challenges.

Who you are spiritually determines the size of the challenge. He had told me that I had to go into the land to inherit the promise. And He was not bothered by the fact that I am a quiet-natured person and I am not a pushy person, because He and I both knew He did not make me a grasshopper. And He has given me the ability to do whatever it is He wants me to do. When the Lord spoke in my spirit to leave Detroit and move to California, I knew I would be facing some new challenges, and He knew fear would not stop me. But I had to follow His leading, because I really did not know what I would be called upon to do. So I had to listen for His directions, because I did not know which way to go.

The Lord had blessed me to meet some of my oldest son's friends on the marine base in Tustin. And I was elated that they received me, when I called them and asked if I could stay with them for a little while, because the Lord was sending me back to California. They were very kind to me. And they graciously adjusted to me praying early in the morning in their home. But I did not know they needed me, until the young man of the house said to me that he was a part of my purpose. He told me that I could have shared this in my first book, but I think now is a better time. After I had been with them a little over a month, he told me that his court martial would begin in February. Then I understood the urgency that the Lord had placed in my spirit to return to California by the end of 1998. The prosecutor asked the court to give him eight years. He and his wife were devastated. I was not moved, because I knew God was a God of mercy from my experience with my oldest son. And I was praying that God would show him mercy too. God granted him mercy, and they gave him six months. I knew from that first incidence, I was moving in the direction and purpose for which the Lord had sent me to California.

Serious Growing Pains

When my own troubles hit in 2002, my children and I were in a battle for our lives. It was not just my son's battle alone; we were all in the fight. And I have learned you're only as strong as your weakest link. I needed all of them to hold on. I needed all of them to believe the Lord was going to bring us through. My mother was concerned about me, because she knows how close I am to all of my children. She was worried about me being in California alone. It had taken her a long time to adjust to my leaving Detroit, and she really wanted me to come back home. But I could not go back, because the Lord was holding me. He had sent me, and He wanted me to stand on His word, because He had something significant for me to do. I had left everything based on His word. I had left a good job, a house, family and friends based on His word. And He had said to me,

> *If any man come to me, and hate not his father, and mother, and wife, and children, and brethren, and sisters, yea, and his own life also, he cannot be my disciple. And whosoever doth not bear his cross, and come after me, cannot be my disciple* (St. Luke 14:26-27).

I could not put anything or anyone before God. Pleasing Him was my ultimate concern. Since He called me, I asked Him to teach me what it meant to be an evangelist. I know what I saw in the church, but I also know what the Bible said concerning Philip, who was led by the Spirit of God. And He has put such a sense of urgency in my spirit, until I have to stay and I cannot look back.

When I sought the Lord for a church home, He led me to a church that presented an enormous set of new challenges for me. Forget about the denominational differences; I started having some serious growing pains. He led me to a church with a congregation of thousands, and the pastor was surrounded by security going and coming. I had never seen that before, so it was quite intimidating to say the least. But the Lord had led me to one of His servants that had the intensity of the gospel to help me get through my hardest trial, because he was a fighter. I discerned that in my spirit. If I wasn't crying, I was shouting (dancing), in spite of the weight of the situation. However, the Lord was renewing my strength at every service; the Lord was sustaining me. And I could hear the Lord clearly, speaking to me through Bishop Jones. When the pastor detected my spirit, he made the comment that God had sent someone there to bless them, and he was praying that they would step up and do whatever it was God had sent them to do. I was experiencing some amazing things. It was astonishing how the Lord had connected my spirit to his spirit.

I tried to join a couple of auxiliaries. I would drive from Newport Beach to Los Angeles trying to attend some meeting, then I had to drive back to Tustin. The driving was wearing me out. And each time I tried to do it, it was such a struggle, so I complained to the Lord. And He simply spoke to my mind, I did not tell you to do that. So I had to stay before Him, in prayer, about His purpose for sending me to this church. I knew He did not intend for me to sit and do nothing. Then He spoke to me again: you have already sung in the choirs; you have already taught Sunday school; you have already been an auxiliary leader. So I knew from that response that He did not send me to continue doing the same things that I had already accomplished in my preparation time.

I really had to seek the Lord for His purpose, and I was as surprised as everyone else when I started writing. The Lord was leading me into my purpose and destiny. When I learned the church was going to be renamed from Greater Bethany to City of Refuge, because of the testimony He had given me concerning my oldest son, I knew it was something He wanted me to share. And He had given me the lead into the manuscript for *When Faith Becomes Glory*. I needed to quote Bishop Jones and use his material, so I knew I needed his permission, because it was his name. Now I had more obstacles, because I was not sure what to do when I really could not talk with him. He is a man of stature and prominence, which can be quite intimidating. And personally, I did not know him and he did not know me. But the Lord had started me writing, and it was flowing. I completed the entire manuscript in three weeks. I was writing in the middle of the night and on weekends.

The Lord had given me something to focus on, in spite of what I was going through, and that was a real blessing. But I still knew I would need Bishop's permission to use his name, before I published the book, plus I needed the money to publish it. And I really didn't want to mention it to him, until I knew everything was in order. So I wasn't even trying to get in his face.

God Does Not Play

But then there were more growing pains on a personal level. A year had passed, and my son still did not have a trial date and I did not understand. I needed to talk with the pastor. I needed some understanding. Now I had been observing how things were being done, and I knew if I wanted to speak with him, I had to do two things. First, I had to get passed being intimidated by who he was; and secondly, I had to swallow my pride and go stand in line to speak with him. I'm telling you, God does not play. He knows our hearts, and He digs deep into the depth of who we are. And He knows how to humble us. But the Lord is so gracious. The particular Sunday when I really felt the pressure and need to talk with the pastor, there wasn't a line, and the Spirit was pushing me. I was tired of crying, but that was my only release because my family was looking to me for strength. I had a real fight with myself that day, and it wasn't all about pride.

I made it up to where Bishop was, as he was trying to get a chair under himself and catch his breath. And I blurted out, "I really need to talk with you." His response was "You know you can't get to me like that." I said, "Oh!" And I turned to walk away, because I didn't know what else to do. I didn't know any of the procedures of this church. I had come from a small church, and I was used to talking with Pastor Anderson anytime. It was a totally different environment. I shut down, just like that. I can shut down easily, but I do not open up quickly. It's that defensive mechanism. And my mind had moved on to questioning God, again, as to why He had led me to this church. Then Bishop said, "Wait a minute, come back." Now I didn't know if I wanted to tell him about my son. But he was so congenial and asked me what the problem was. He exhibited his gentle side as he tried to get me to open back up and tell him what was wrong. Once I realized I could tell him, I disclosed my son's situation to him. He asked me if he was guilty. I said "Yes, he's guilty, but that is not my problem. I'm looking to God for mercy on that issue." I needed to understand if it was legal for them to keep him in a county jail over a year and not have a trial. I did not know anything about the kind of situation I was dealing with. I did not know what time frames were reasonable, but I knew that being in jail over a year without a trial seemed unreasonable to me. We talked those few minutes, and I felt better, and I did not need anything else from him. From that encounter, I knew God had given me a pastor. The next day, as I reflected on those few moments even before I published my first book, God gave me *A Shepherd's Heart*. More importantly, He had taught me through that little exercise that He wanted me to stay open to His leading, even if I had to push my way through it. As He was changing certain dispositions that I have, He was strengthening me for the long haul.

Shortly thereafter, I found a publisher, and the book was ready to go. I paid the initial one-third installment payment, and the turnaround time was real quick. I had the first proofs within a couple of weeks. I still did not want to talk to Bishop about the book project, until I knew

I had a reasonable completion date. But also, I was praying to God and telling Him, "Lord, what if I put my money out there and he will not grant me permission to use his name?" The Lord was not making this easy for me, even though He told me to do it. I was connected to Him, and I was hearing His word. I kept hearing Him say, "You do not need anyone's permission to do what I have called you to do." I understood that, but I would say to the Lord, "I cannot use someone's name without their permission." I knew the right thing to do, and I was trying to go about things in the proper manner. Then the Lord would send some messages to just whip me, and I was crying about that, but I did not know what to do. And I did not have anyone I could talk to about the situation who would understand me, because I already sounded crazy to some of my family and friends. So it was God dealing with me, and He was stretching me to the limit, and He does not have limits. I struggled to move away from the scripture with which God whips me the most. Sometimes I am not there, but other times I must be. Whenever I hear certain messages preached from the Book of Timothy, I feel a sting. However, I published *When Faith Becomes Glory* in June 2004, and the Lord covered me. So I presented it to Bishop Jones, and he received the gift that God had given me to share. And I am grateful for the privilege and opportunity that God has given me to sow into the lives of others.

CHAPTER 3

Sowing for Change

The Lord had led me to a church where He would sustain me by the power of His word and, where He would constantly challenge me to keep moving forward, even in the midst of my trials. I had written the first book, *When Faith Becomes Glory*, and it was reprinted within one year of its release. But the Spirit pushed me to continue writing, so I immediately started writing the manuscript for *A Shepherd's Heart*. The Lord was redeeming the time as He had promised. He had given me a vision, and I was beginning to produce something of significance. It was overwhelming, but I kept pressing on. The Lord taught me that not only did He want me to flow in the Holy Spirit but with the spirit of the pastor. He had made me sensitive to Bishop Jones' spirit, which is not only intense but one of consideration of others and vision.

I was standing in my kitchen, washing some greens, and the Lord put in my spirit to start a company. I asked Him, "For what?"

He responded, "You need a bucket for Me to pour into."

I said, "Lord, You're pushing me really hard." I questioned Him about it again, because somehow we have these dialogues in my mind. So He brought this story to my mind:

> *Now there cried a certain woman of the wives of the sons of the prophets unto Elisha, saying, Thy servant my husband is dead; and thou knowest that thy servant did fear the* LORD*: and the creditor is come to take unto him my two sons to be bondmen. And Elisha said unto her, What shall I do for thee? tell me, what hast thou in the house? And she said, Thine handmaid hath not any thing in the house, save a pot of oil. Then he said, Go, borrow thee vessels abroad of all thy neighbours, even empty vessels; borrow not a few. And when thou art come in, thou shalt shut the door upon thee and upon thy sons, and shalt pour out into all those vessels, and thou shalt set aside that which is full. So she went from him, and shut the door upon her and upon her sons, who brought the vessels to her; and she poured out. And it came to pass, when the vessels were full, that she said unto her son, Bring me yet a vessel. And he said unto her, There is not a vessel more. And the oil stayed* (2 Kings 4:1-6).

And whenever God speaks His word in my spirit, that settles everything for me. So now, my only question was, how am I supposed to do that? I tell you, God is so awesome. I cannot really describe how or what He does, although I am trying. I said okay, but I did not know what to do. As I was going about my normal Saturday routine, I stopped by a friend's house to visit. And I told her about the Lord telling me to start a business because He needed a bucket to pour into. I told her, "I do not know why He tells me these things, knowing that I do not know many people here in California."

She said, "Well, speak to my husband and maybe he can introduce you to our tax man who set up my daycare." So I did. And he agreed to make an appointment for me with his friend, and he also agreed to meet me at his office to introduce us. The tax guy just happened to be Jewish. I told him what I wanted do, and he asked me if I had a name selected for the company. I said yes. The Lord had given me to name it *Vessels of Honor*. He asked me if I just had to have that name and why. And I relayed to him what it meant. He gave me some advice, which I agreed to. But after doing a search for the name, he found there were some churches and other ministries with the same name. He said he would look up the word *vessels* in Hebrew to see if he could find another word, since I was determined to use it. But he found out it simply meant *bucket*, and he said I couldn't name it Buckets of Honor. I said, no, but that is what God told me I needed, some buckets for Him to pour into. And since I would not change the name, we went with VOH, LLC (Vessels of Honor); I could still use that. So that was done. Then the Lord said it was time to build a website, so I called another friend and told her that I needed a website. She is a jewel, and she was excited about being a part of what the Lord was doing in my life. We spent about three weekends working on it. She put everything together, and all I had to do was the writing of what I wanted to say out on the web. And we published it. I keep saying God is a wonder! And He is so worthy of all the praise and honor that I can give Him. I do not know why He has been gracious to me, but I truly thank Him for every experience. He keeps on blessing me, and I thank Him.

Don't Faint

Then Bishop preached *Don't Faint.*[3] The message came at a critical time, because although the Lord was moving me forward in the midst of the storm in my life, I was getting tired. He took his text from Psalm 126:5-6:

> *They that sow in tears shall reap in joy. He that goeth forth and weepeth, bearing precious seed, shall doubtless come again with rejoicing, bringing his sheaves with him.*

Galatians 6:6-9 reads,

> *Let him that is taught in the word communicate unto him that teacheth in all good things.*

He said, "So there is reciprocity between the teacher and the person who is taught."

> *Be not deceived; God is not mocked: for whatsoever a man soweth, that shall he also reap. For he that soweth to his flesh shall of the flesh reap corruption; but he that soweth to the Spirit shall of the Spirit reap life everlasting. And let us not be weary in well doing: for in due season we shall reap, if we faint not.*

He said,

> "Touch somebody and tell them, 'Don't Faint. Whatever you do, don't faint!' A couple of things are interesting here, particularly, when you deal with the concept of reaping. It is what you set in motion that, ultimately, comes back to you. And it's critical to grasp this, because whenever God speaks, He speaks something into existence and whatever He speaks into existence, He provides

a seed. And it is here, where God shares with us His omnipotence and His power. Because He speaks something into existence, and then He supplies a seed in whatever He speaks. He now allows you the privilege to indulge yourself in what it is He has done, because the power of the seed now is in your hand. Notice what He does, He speaks it into existence; He puts in it a seed, and then He allows us the privilege to share in His power by perpetuating whatever He put in existence in giving us the seed. So God speaks and I sow.

"When I sow, I now participate in the power of God, because He allows me the privilege to operate within what He is doing, and He gives me, then, the strength to continue something that He has started. I cannot speak it into existence, He speaks it into existence, and then He allows me to share with what He does. It's critical to see this now; that whatever, He speaks into existence has the power to continue, until He stops. And whatever I sow has the power to continue, until I stop sowing. Now notice, oftentimes, we are looking for our lives to change, but if our lives are going to change, we have to sow different things for different things to result. It is a simple truth, but it's tied so much into God's omnipotence that the writer in Galatians says, "Don't be deceived, God is not mocked, whatsoever a man sows, that shall he also reap" which means that, you can't reverse what you have already put into motion, it's got to work itself out. It's got to work itself through, and while the negative is working itself through, you can't sow negative and expect positive. You have to while the negative is working itself through, begin to plant seeds of the positive in order for the cycle to change. If you look in our lives, many times, we have gone around in the same circle, and oftentimes, we do the same things; it's just a different face, a different person, a different situation, a different place. But we, generally, end up in the same situation because we sow the same things. And what God is saying to us is I have put some things in motion that I will not reverse; you have to take the initiative to reverse your circumstance, by doing things a little bit differently.

Follow My Lead

"There is a general principal that God has placed, that He will not change, and He will not go around. And that is, whatever, I put out, I will get it back. And it is so fixed because it is such a part of God, that there is no way for any one of us to do one thing and expect something else to happen. And so now, I have the power to control my tomorrow by what I do today. I can't do something that's off and expect something on to come about. I have to do what's on, to get what's on. And what God is saying to me now is I have given you, then, the strength to determine what your future is going to be. And you will not sit around and cry to me about what your tomorrow is, because I'm putting in your hands the ability to fix your tomorrow. All I want you to do is follow my lead and follow my principle and lay out there what it is you want for your tomorrow. You can't lay out sadness and depression and not expect it tomorrow. You cannot lay out the negative and expect the positive. You cannot lay out what is bad and expect something good. God says, I'm going to move you into a place of strength, but I'm going to give you the principle by which you will have a better tomorrow.

"It is interesting because when I note this I see that God's liberality is expressed, then, in His ability to release to me the strength to do what I need to do. And I can't sit around and allow other people to determine my future. I have to take my life in my own hands. I have to look beyond where I am today into what I want tomorrow. And I can't allow other people to determine how I operate. I have to allow God to set the seed in me and give me the power to move my tomorrow to where it should be. If I'm struggling today, it's because I sowed something negative yesterday. If I'm having a fight today, it's because yesterday I did not operate in the line that God gave me. I just refused to do His will and refused to follow where He would lead. And so, consequently, now I am suffering because of some negatives yesterday. But every day that God gives me, He gives me another opportunity to change what yesterday is bringing. No zeal then, no zeal! No matter how ardent I am, no matter how I pray, no matter how fervent my prayers are, no matter how I profess God, no matter how loud I get, I cannot impose on God to do differently than what I have sown. No matter how I sing, no matter how many prayer partners I get, no matter how we hold each others hands and touch and agree, if, I have not sown what is proper, I cannot reap what is proper.

"Oftentimes, we're looking for a miracle breakthrough, but the miracle, God says, is in your hand. I have not put it up to chance. I have not allowed somebody else to determine how you come out. God has allowed me the privilege to control my tomorrow. If God has allowed you to control your tomorrow, then you should rejoice because He is not leaving your life to chance. What He's saying to you is, if you follow my lead and if I order your steps and if you will not rebel against the ordering of your steps, then I can make your tomorrow through your own hands exactly what you want it to be. I feel like God is doing me a favor when He allows me to determine how my tomorrow comes out, by giving me His principle. And He's saying now, that my principle is so wrapped up in my omnipotence, that there is no devil in hell that can bring you bad results, when you sow good things. There is no enemy that can step in here and destroy what you have presented, because once you walk in my principle, the enemy is completely helpless. The only time we will give the enemy strength is when we walk outside the principles of God. And we expect some hocus-pocus to take place, and it's not going to happen. Once I do the will of God, it's going to bring good results. And there is nobody who can stop God from blessing me, once I have done what God has ordained.

Sowing Into Destiny

"It is essential here to grasp this, because now He gives us two main areas. One area is carnal and the other is spiritual. So now, then, I have to look within the things of faith to understand that there is something in my spirit that needs to be sown, that's going to multiply spiritual blessings. The first thing is, if, I move into the flesh, I'm looking for quick responses. And generally, flesh gives you quick responses, but they're not sustainable. Because no matter how much you satisfy flesh, it needs gratification the next minute. No matter how much you give flesh, flesh will always be empty, because flesh needs to feed quickly and it responds quickly to the stimuli. When I sow spiritually, now I'm sowing into destiny, because now I am sowing into the things of God that orchestrate and control my whole being. When I sow to flesh, I'm really just responding to what flesh is calling for, and there is no direction, no sustainable power when you deal with flesh. Why? Because flesh is leading to death; flesh is dying every day. When I sow into the spirit, now I sow into the destiny and the purpose of God, because it's in my spirit God has placed my destiny and my purpose. It is in my spirit that He gives me the revelation of what He wants me to be, and He forces me to move into the spirit to gain the things of God.

"You will find that, whenever you begin to move into the things of the spirit that the flesh will always fight, because the flesh does not want permanence. It does not want to be brought under the control of the power of the spirit. What the flesh wants is to go around in quick fixes and quick responses, immediate responses to its demand. It's a sort of rainbow chasing; it's a quick thrill kind of a thing that I'm just looking for gratification real fast, but I don't want any permanence. What God is saying is I want to bring you to permanence. I want to bring you to a place where you don't have to worry about what's happening the next minute. You have already decided what will happen the next minute, and Satan can't do a thing about it. This is why the devil wants you up and down, vacillating, and in and out. He wants you moving without any real certainty or any positiveness, because once the devil has you jumping up and down, he dictates how your life goes. But what the Lord says is if you jump out of the flesh into the spirit, then you can set your destiny that no devil can break. And the devil wants you under his control, but God wants you under the control of the power of who you are, so that no matter what's going on outside, I have the inner feeling and power that victory shall be mine, because I've sown the kind of thing that will bring the results that God requires of me.

"Oftentimes, when you're dealing with the flesh it's like dealing with an individual who never has long-term relationships. Whenever you go long term, first of all, you have to be fair because anybody who is unfair in any relationship, it will soon come to a close. You've got to be fair in your dealing. If I'm dealing with you and I realize that we have this deal going on, I will say to you, that this is not fair. And because I realize that sooner or later I might have the advantage, but the advantage won't be there for long because you're going to wake up and say this is not in my favor. The flesh is like that, it does not deal with long term relationships. What it does is, it takes pennies now and it ignores dollars later. That's the flesh! The flesh wants quick gratification and it breaks up its relationships because flesh is not fair, it's selfish. When you deal in the Spirit of God, then you deal with a God who sets things up for eternity. And when God sets things up for eternity, then He wants you to walk in what is fair. If I give you, then you give me back. And you give me back what I require of you, because I had to give you strength in order for you to respond to me.

Don't Lose Heart

"Now, when an individual begins to react to God, the tendency now is to get tired, because the flesh and the enemy will pull against you to break down your courage to wait for God to give you what He has promised, because the flesh is saying it ought to come quickly. But what God is saying is, if you hang in there with the courage, and if you don't lose heart, I will set you up in a place where you will never lack again. It is here where the flesh wants to fight. And somebody says, how do I get weary doing the right thing? Well, I get weary because the enemy comes after me more intensely than ever before, because he wants to break the cycle that I have begun. He realizes that if he can break me down in the sowing period, then he can break me down for the harvest. Because if I stop you from sowing or cause you to change the direction of what you are doing, then I will guarantee that you will not have the harvest in the end. Ah! That's why when you decide to walk with God it looks like everything goes crazy around you. Because the devil wants to break you down and cause you to lose heart so that you will not wait, until the Lord brings to pass what you have sowed and believed Him for. But don't be faint hearted. What God declares will come to pass, if you just hang in there with everything you have. It's got to come to pass!

"The harvest, then, is not immediate. The flesh is looking for immediate but the spirit understands that, even though I don't see it coming about, I have sowed the seed and it's got to rise up. It is here then that the vision pushes you, because the vision has got to keep you going, in order for it to come to pass. I sow but I don't sow and sit around looking at the seed in the ground. I sow but I'm looking at what God is going to bring because of my action. And so now, the vision then pushes me; it will not stop. It does not let me quit, because the vision is ever before me of what God is going to bring to pass in my life. The vision then causes me to hold on. And even though I speak and declare it, I look and believe it, and no matter how rough things are, I have sown and I will wait for God to bring it to pass. The thing that you're expecting God to do is so great that it takes time to bring it to pass. He spoke it, you sow it, but in the sowing you have to go through the seasons, in order for the harvest to come. It does not mean that it is not coming to pass. It just simply means you've got to believe God by faith to sow it, and you have to believe God to reap it. You can't flip around with satanic movements and believe that you're going to get what God requires. Because what God says to you is a double-minded man is unstable in all his ways. You can't start something and let the devil talk you out of it, but you've got to hold your ground and believe God to fulfill what He said. Tell your neighbor, don't faint! Don't faint!

"You see, immediate harvest means no effort. And life lived under spirit control means it takes effort, because you've got to fight how you feel. Because many times, you don't feel like it's going to come to pass. It's not about what you feel; it's about what you believe. And if God declared it's coming to pass, it's coming to pass. It's got to come to pass! I sowed it and I'm waiting on it. It's got to come to pass. I trusted God when I stepped out, and I trust God every day! I believe it, and there's nothing that the devil can do that can stop it from coming to pass.

"When the spirit controls, then the Spirit of God brings you into stability. And the Spirit of God allows you a place where you can find comfort while you wait. Much of the time, my pain comes when I don't move into the spirit and allow God to comfort me in the power of His presence. Because it's in the presence of God I revive my strength. It's in the presence of God that I renew my power to continue. Because once I have moved into the things of God and the enemy attacks, then I have to allow the spirit to control or work out the future that I have placed in God's hands. Because once I did the right thing, and once I operated in the right manner, I've got to wait for God to bring it to pass. I don't have to take things in my own hands, because He has an omnipotent declaration that whatever you sow, you're going to reap.

"I don't have to take folks and their attitudes in my hands. I don't have to respond by the way they treat me. Because whatever they put out to me that is negative before God, it's going to come back to them. Pray for them that despitefully use you. And the reason you pray for them is because what's about to happen in their life, oh God! You don't bother the child of God who has sown the right thing before God, because you'll get it back the same way you put it out. And, because I know it's coming back to you, instead of wanting it to happen, I say, Lord, give my brother grace and give him mercy.

"It is here, then, that the Spirit of God must power me, because oftentimes I will react to how I'm being treated while I'm waiting on God to bring it to pass, and this is another ploy of the devil. He wants me to react negatively to how I'm treated, because he realizes it's not how I'm treated that will determine my future; it's how I react to how I'm treated. Because now, I began to sow seeds of vengeance, but the Lord told me, don't revenge. He told me, vengeance is mine, I will repay. Be good to folk who are evil to you, because their being evil to you can't stop you from being blessed.

Self-denial

"So the effort, then, of giving to the spirit is the effort that comes with self-denial, which is difficult in and of itself. Because sowing, now, means I'm sowing myself.

I'm sowing all that I am, and I'm not sowing to the negative. I'm sowing to the positive. So it's sowing what you do, and you don't have to have anything but you to sow the right spirit before God; to sow the right attitude towards others; to sow the right disposition, as you move in and out of your job; to sow the right spirit in your home. And what God says is, as you sow yourself, it is an investment of you that's going to bring back constant blessing; goodness and mercy is going to follow you, wherever you go. Because I have sown the best of myself, I have not allowed the evil in me to come out, but I've denied the evil, and I've sown the good, and I've got to be blessed. Because God promises, whatever I sow that shall I also reap. Oh, I'm getting ready to tell you, that the rest of my life is going to be better than the first of my life, because I've done what God has required.

"It is here then, when I sow myself, I sow mind and attitude and even money. Then vision diminishes what is not fulfilled immediately, because now I've got to wait for it. I've got to learn now to be good for goodness' sake. I've got to be driven to bless others or driven to show other people that God is on my side. I don't operate now simply out of reward, because now I've had to wait long enough to become used to giving of myself. You see, here is the power that God wants to translate us in. He wants me to be good for goodness' sake, not just for reward, but to be good because good is a part of who I am. He wants me to be kind, not looking for anything back. He wants me to sow kindness, just out of what I am; that's what the waiting period is about. He wants me to express what I am, from the spirit of who I am, not selfishly, but completely and totally, because that's who I am. I've gotten to the place now where I don't have to argue because that's not who I am. I've gotten to the place where I don't have to debate it because that's not who I am. I don't have to sit and be caught betwixt whether or not, I'm going to hurt you or be good to you because that's not who I am. I've waited long enough for what I have sown, that I can't help but be who I am. And, I can't help but receive what God has in store for me. Oh, don't be weary, don't back up, don't quit being who you are. Don't quit being kind, don't quit being sweet, don't quit being the strength that God has called you to be.

I'm Growing Every Day

"It is here now, He says, that as a result of being who you are, I'm going to let things flow like I want them to flow, because I have commanded it, it's got to come to pass. The motive is purified, now, by character development. I'm not doing it just to receive; I'm doing it because that's the way I am. I have become what God has required, and I put out what God wants me to do. Prolonging the response then leads to character growth, because while I'm waiting, I'm growing. I'm growing every day! While I'm waiting for God to bring it to pass, I'm fighting with the tendency to give up, because I should have given up by now. But it's become so much a part of me that I can't help but express it right now. I'm not just doing this to be paid; I'm doing this because it's me. And if, you do nothing for me, I'll still be good to you! It's just me now! I've started some things in motion that I cannot stop any longer because it's just a part of me now. Blessing, I'll bless you; touching, I'll bless you; speaking, I'll bless you. Because it's become a part of me, which means now I'm walking in the power of God, in spite of satanic opposition. He will not break me down. He will not cause me to ask why. I will stand in the place where God has put me. And I will not get tired, but I will hold onto what God requires, until the breakthrough comes.

"The words be weary are used of husbandmen who are tempted to slacken their exercise, by reason of weariness that's caused by a prolonged effort. It's not enough just to sow to the flesh; it's not enough to struggle with the vision; it's not enough to deal only with character development, but you've got to stay alive, until the season comes. My season is about to take place, and I can't quit before it comes into fact. I've got to keep on being who I am. I can't allow myself to change, because I'm created unto good works. No glory, no disappointment! I'm God's workmanship, and He has made us. It is He who has given me the power to overcome everything the devil throws my way. And I've got to hang in there until the blessing of God begins to move in my favor. I'm doing what's right to do, and as long as I'm doing the right thing, there's nothing the enemy can do about it. Somebody's in a struggle right now. And you feel like you've done all that you can do. And here's what God is saying: you've done all you can do, but I'm going to do the rest in you. And you will not back up, neither will you quit. You will not stop now, because I'm getting ready to open the windows of heaven and pour you out every blessing that I promised I would pour you out. You can't stop now, because I see a cloud the size of a man's hand! It's getting ready to rain in your life.

"The devil is upset with you, because he's tried to turn you into the kind of person that would be evil and wicked and he hasn't been able to do it. This is why he's pulling out every stop trying to get you to feel like God will not bring your blessing to pass. Because what the devil wants you to do is quit walking the way you've been walking. And he wants you to turn another way, but the devil is a liar. The truth is never in him. What's about to happen in your life is a breakthrough that has never been seen before. And what the devil wants you to do is block it from coming to pass, by changing your disposition. But God told me to tell you, don't faint now. You're too close to let go right now. It's about to happen for you. Don't reverse it! God has already reversed my curse, and I'm not getting ready to turn it back around. I'm going to hold my place; I'm going to hold my praise; I'm going to lift Him up like never before. I'm going to hold my grace; hold my right attitude. I'm going to give God the glory no matter how people make me feel, because in due season I'm going to reap, if, I faint not! I've been good for so long, I'm enjoying it! I've praised God for so long, I'm enjoying it! I've lifted Him up for so long, I'm enjoying it! And the victory shall be mine!

"Don't quit right now; keep on being good; keep on being kind; keep on praising God; keep on holding on. It's getting ready to happen; it's getting ready to come to pass. My blessing, I've already sown it, and I'm getting ready to harvest. Somebody said I was stupid to be so good. The devil is a liar; look and see what God is getting ready to do. Call me stupid when it's harvest time. When the blessing began to flow, let's hear what they call you then. Blessed! Upright! Favored of the Lord! I held on! I knew He would answer! I knew He would bless me! I knew He would bring it to pass. For every time they pulled on you, every time they grabbed you, every time you had to give up something, it's coming back to you more than you ever thought. You will be happy; you will be blessed; you will have the victory. He's going to double it and send it back, shaken together, pressed down and running over."

Bishop Jones preached that message in the middle of my hardest trial, when I was having a real tough time. There were times when my pain was so great, I actually ran out of the service and fell down in the foyer crying out to God for mercy. Then there were other times when I would run around the church, just from the pure joy of His word, because I have learned that the joy of the Lord is my strength! This is the United States of America, and we have a constitution and laws that say we have certain rights, which many times are denied. And I had no one to turn to for help but God. I was tired, but the word of God came and lifted my spirit.

CHAPTER 4

Love Digs Deep

As I stated at the beginning, I was born in a very significant time in history and many people from the past have influenced my life. I was a little girl when Mrs. Rosa Parks refused to give up her seat to a white man on a bus in Montgomery, Alabama. Her quiet act of defiance changed the course of history in the United States and initiated the Civil Rights Movement. And as I entered into adulthood, many horrendous things were happening in our nation. I lived through President John F. Kennedy being assassinated; I lived through his brother Senator Robert F. Kennedy being assassinated. Those were terrible times. I lived through the 1967 riots in Detroit, and I saw the National Guard patrolling my neighborhood as the city was on fire.

But there was still another voice in history; there was yet another preacher whose words penetrated my spirit. He was the late Dr. Martin Luther King, Jr. And he has left a legacy and a message that is still relevant for all of us today. Dr.

King preached this sermon on February 4, 1968, from the pulpit of Ebenezer Baptist Church.[4] I cannot quote the entire sermon, but I pray you will remember and reflect on the hope that he endeavored to give to us. So please, open your hearts and minds and receive his words.

The Drum Major Instinct

> "This morning I would like to use as a subject from which to preach 'The Drum Major Instinct.' And our text for the morning is taken from a very familiar passage in the tenth chapter as recorded by Saint Mark; beginning with the thirty-fifth verse of that chapter, we read these words: And James and John the sons of Zebedee came unto him saying, 'Master, we would that thou shouldest do for us whatsoever we shall desire.' And he said unto them, 'what would ye that I should do for you?' And they said unto him, 'Grant unto us that we may sit one on the right hand and the other on thy left hand in thy glory.' But Jesus said unto them, ye know not what ye ask. Can ye drink of the cup that I drink of, and be baptized with the baptism that I am baptized with?' And they said unto him, "We can." And Jesus said unto them, 'Ye shall indeed drink of the cup that I drink of, and with the baptism that I am baptized withal shall ye be baptized. But to sit on my right hand and on my left hand is not mine to give, but it shall be given to them for whom it is prepared.'
>
> "And then, Jesus goes on toward the end of that passage to say, 'But so shall it not be among you, but whosoever will be great among you, shall be your servant; and whosoever of you will be the chiefest, shall be servant of all.'

"The setting is clear. James and John are making a specific request of the master. They had dreamed, as most Hebrews dreamed, of a coming king of Israel who would set Jerusalem free. And establish his kingdom on Mount Zion, and in righteousness rule the world. And they thought of Jesus as this kind of king, and they were thinking of that day when Jesus would reign supreme as this new king of Israel. And they were saying now, 'when you establish your kingdom, let one of us sit on the right hand and the other on the left hand of your throne.'

Basic Desires

"Now very quickly, we would automatically condemn James and John, and we would say they were selfish. Why would they make such a selfish request? But before we condemn them too quickly, let us look calmly and honestly at ourselves, and we will discover that we too have those same basic desires for recognition, for importance, that same desire for attention, that same desire to be first. Of course, the other disciples got mad with James and John, and you could understand why, but we must understand that we have some of the same James and John qualities. There is deep down within all of us an instinct. It's a kind of drum major instinct—a desire to be out front, a desire to lead the parade, a desire to be first. And it is something that runs a whole gamut of life.

"And so before we condemn them, let us see that we all have the drum major instinct. We all want to be important, to surpass others, to achieve distinction, to lead the parade. Alfred Adler, the great psychoanalyst, contends that this is the dominant impulse. Sigmund Freud used to contend that sex was the dominant impulse, and Adler came with a new argument saying that this quest for recognition, this desire for attention, this desire for distinction is the basic impulse, the basic drive of human life—this drum major instinct.

"And you know we begin early to ask life to put us first. Our first cry as a baby was a bid for attention. And all through childhood, the drum major impulse or instinct is a major obsession. Children ask life to grant them first place. They are a little bundle of ego. And they have innately the drum major impulse, or the drum major instinct.

"Now in adult life, we still have it, and we really never get by it. We like to do something good. And you know we like to be praised for it. Now if you don't believe that, you just go on living life and you will discover very soon that you like to be praised. Everybody likes it, as a matter of fact. And somehow this warm glow we feel when we are praised, or when our name is in print, is something of the vitamin A to our ego. Nobody is unhappy when they are praised, even if they know they don't deserve it, and even if they don't believe it. The only unhappy people about praise, is when that praise is going too much toward somebody else. But everybody likes to be praised, because of this real drum major instinct.

"Now the presence of the drum major instinct is why so many people are joiners. You know there are some people who just join everything. And it's really a quest for attention, and recognition, and importance. And they get names that give them that impression. So you get your groups, and they become the grand patron, and the little fellow who is henpecked at home needs a chance to be the most worthy, of the most worthy of something. It is the drum major impulse and longing that runs the gamut of human life. And so we see it everywhere, this quest for recognition. And we join things, over-join really, that we think that we will find that recognition in.

A Dangerous, Pernicious Instinct

"There comes a time that the drum major instinct can become destructive. And that's where I want to move now. I want to move to the point of saying that if this instinct is not harnessed, it becomes a very dangerous, pernicious instinct. For instance, if it isn't harnessed, it causes one's personality to become distorted. I guess that's the most damaging aspect of it—what it does to the personality. If it isn't harnessed, you will end up day in and day out trying to deal with your ego problem by boasting.

"Have you ever heard people that—you know, and I'm sure you've met them—that really become sickening because they just sit up all the time talking about themselves. And they just boast, and boast, and boast, and that's the person who has not harnessed the drum major instinct.

"And then it does other things to the personality. It causes you to lie about who you know sometimes. There are some people who are influence peddlers. And in their attempt to deal with the drum major instinct, they have to try to identify with the so-called big name people. And if you're not careful, they will make you think they know somebody that they don't really know. They know them well, they sip tea with them. And they...this and that; that...that happens to people.

"And the other thing is that it causes one to engage ultimately in activities that are merely used to get attention. Criminologists tell us that some people are driven to crime because of this drum major instinct. They don't feel that they are getting enough attention through the normal channels of social behavior, and others turn to anti-social behavior in order to get attention, in order to feel important. And so they get that gun. And before they know it, they rob the bank in a quest for recognition, in a quest for importance.

"And then, the final great tragedy of the distorted personality is the fact that when one fails to harness this instinct, he ends by trying to push others down in order to push himself up. And whenever you do that, you engage in some of the most vicious activities. You will spread evil, vicious, lying gossip on people, because you are trying to pull them down in order to push yourself up. And the great issue of life is to harness the drum major instinct.

Don't Give Up This Instinct

"When the church is true to its nature, it says, 'Whosoever will, let him come.' And it does not propose to satisfy the perverted uses of the drum major instinct. It's the one place where everybody should be the same, standing before a common master and savior. And a recognition grows out of this, that all men are brothers because they are children of a common father.

"The drum major instinct can lead to exclusivism in one's thinking, can lead one to feel that because he has some training, he's a little better than that person that doesn't have it, or because he has some economic security, that he's a little better than the person who doesn't have it. And that's the uncontrolled, perverted use of the drum major instinct."

I cannot give you the fullness of his message, although all of it is so good. I have to skip to what I found to be another point.

Dr. King said,

"And we have perverted the drum major instinct. But let me rush on to my conclusion, because I want you to see what Jesus was really saying. What was the answer that Jesus gave these men? It's very interesting. One would have thought that Jesus would have said, 'You are out of your place. You are selfish. Why would you raise such a question?'

"But that isn't what Jesus did. He did something altogether different. He said in substance, 'Oh, I see you want to be first. You want to be great. You want to be important. You want to be significant. Well you ought to be. If you're going to be My disciple, you must be.' But He reordered priorities. And He said, 'Yes, don't give up this instinct. It's a good instinct if you use it right. It's a good instinct if you don't distort it and pervert it. Don't give it up. Keep feeling the need for being important. Keep feeling the need for being first. But I want you to be first in love. I want you to be first in moral excellence. I want you to be first in generosity. That is what I want you to do.'

"And he transformed the situation by giving a new definition of greatness. And you know how he said it? He said now, 'Brethren, I can't give you greatness. And really, I can't make you first.' This is what Jesus said to James and John. 'You must earn it. True greatness comes not by favoritism, but by fitness. And the right hand and the left are not Mine to give; they belong to those who are prepared.'

"And so, Jesus gave us a new norm of greatness. If you want to be important, wonderful; If you want to be recognized, wonderful; If you want to be great, wonderful. But recognize that he who is greatest among you shall be your servant. That's your new definition of greatness. And this morning, the thing that I like about it...by giving that definition of greatness, it means that everybody can be great, because everybody can serve. You don't have to have a college degree to serve. You don't have to make your subject and your verb agree to serve. You don't have to know about Plato and Aristotle to serve. You don't have to know Einstein's theory of relativity to serve. You don't have to know the second theory of thermodynamics in physics to serve. You only need a heart full of grace. A soul generated by love. And you can be that servant...

"Nineteen centuries have come and gone, and today, He stands as the most influential figure that ever entered human history. All of the armies that ever marched, all the navies that ever sailed, all the parliaments that ever sat, and all the kings that ever reigned put together have not affected the life of man on this earth, as much as that one solitary life. His name may be a familiar one. But today I can hear them talking about Him. Every now and then somebody says, 'He's King of kings.' And again I can hear somebody saying, 'He's Lord of lords.' Somewhere else I can hear somebody saying, 'In Christ there is no East, nor West,' And they go on and talk about...'In Him there's no North and South, but one great fellowship of love throughout the whole wide world.' He didn't have anything. He just went around serving and doing good!

"This morning, you can be on His right hand and His left if you serve. It's the only way in.

"And that's all I want to say...if I can help somebody as I pass along, if I can cheer somebody with a word or song, if I can show somebody he's traveling wrong, then my living will not be in vain. If I can do my duty as a Christian ought, if I can bring salvation to a world once wrought, if I can spread the message as the Master taught, then my living will not be in vain.

"Yes, Jesus, I want to be on Your right side or Your left side, not for any selfish reason. I want to be on Your right or Your best side, not in terms of some political kingdom or ambition, but I just want to be there in love and in justice and in truth and in commitment to others, so that we can make of this old world a new world."

The enemy stole the life of this great warrior too, but Dr. King's dream of freedom, equal rights and justice still lives on, and his legacy still lives on. He, too, pointed us to Jesus, as our chief example of a servant and as the author and finisher of our faith. So I am endeavoring with everything within me not to let his dream die. Because of Mrs. Rosa Parks, I was not forced to ride at the back of the bus or give up my seat to anyone, except by choice. And because of all of those who stood up for our inalienable, rights given to us by the Declaration of Independence, doors of opportunity were opened. Although I did not go through the doors of the universities, I never forgot my dreams and aspirations of doing something meaningful with my life. Dr. Martin Luther King, Jr., President John Kennedy and his brother Senator Robert Kennedy were my twentieth-century examples of what it means to lose your life for a cause.

But I'm so glad that they could not take Jesus' life. He laid it down for me. And the really good thing is that He rose again that I might have life.

As the Father knoweth me, even so know I the Father: and I lay down my life for the sheep. And other sheep I have, which are not of this fold: them also I must bring, and they shall hear my voice; and there shall be one fold, and one shepherd. Therefore doth my Father love me, because I lay down my life, that I might take it again. No man taketh it from me, but I lay it down of myself. I have power to lay it down, and I have power to take it again. This commandment have I received of my Father (St. John 10:15-16).

And because Jesus had the power to rise up from the grave, He has restored life unto me.

Chapter 5

Crossing the Finish Line

The Lord had blessed me to become a responsible adult and to be a good mother. He also gave me good work ethics, and I thought that was all there was. Again, when I was seeking Him for a church home, He directed me to the City of Refuge. And not only did I see things that were surprising to me, I heard the words, "You're gifted." I had heard a lot of things, but I had never heard that. Then Bishop said that we need to search ourselves and ask God to show us what He had buried in us to give Him glory. I was already seeking God for His purpose for directing me to this church, but when I started writing, it started flowing. And it has continued to flow into three books. That's God! God did that! And He is more than amazing, He is awesome. Apparently, this is what He sent me to do. He excavated deep and uncovered the treasure He had buried within me. He blew past the sand of my being young and naïve, He dug through the hardness left from my feelings of rejection and failure, and when He got to the stable rock of faith that He had planted within me, He cultivated the ground of my heart with His love. So I worship Him! And I praise Him for all the marvelous things He has done in my life. There is nobody like Him! And He alone deserves all the glory, the honor and the praise! And I, willingly, give it to Him.

You're Expected to Win

The Lord gave Bishop Jones a message entitled *You're Expected to Win*,[5] taken from Hebrews 12:1-3. And since this is a book of apologetics, I want you to understand that once you have entered the race, you have to run until the end! You need to hold on until the end! It does not matter your placing, just keep going until you cross the finish line. Bishop Jones preached and said,

> "The first three verses is actually an exaltation to faith and to godliness. It is critical, because the psychological disposition of the Hebrew at this point was at an all-time low. And they were at an all-time low because they expected the Lord to come quickly and vindicate the fact that they had walked away from their Judaism and they followed the carpenter's son from Nazareth. And they were being ridiculed, because He did not bring into fruition or completion the reason for their walking away from Judaism. That is, He did not culminate their salvation as quickly as they wanted Him to and lead them into heaven as quickly as they wanted Him to. Because they needed that, to offset the disposition of those who thought they were foolish to walk away from Judaism to follow this carpenter's son from Nazareth. Can you

imagine the intensity of that day, because even to this day, they have not yet, as a whole, received Jesus as the Messiah. So in those days, when they were moving from Judaism into Christianity and the Lord did not come quickly, then it caused them to back up and to go back into Judaism. And the Judaizers were pushing it so vehemently and so vociferously that they were shaking in instability because the Lord would not come quickly.

"Now it's critical to understand that, because anytime we're in a battle and we're seeking to achieve a certain height in God, and we take the risk of stepping out of what normal people do, and we move away from our traditional roots, many of us want quick results, because quick results says that I made the right decision. But when the Lord stands back and does not move quickly to give you vindication or to indicate that you are right, now your faith is being stretched like an elastic, 'cause now I am to believe God in spite of the ridicule, in spite of the opposition, in spite of how slow things seem to be coming to pass. All of us have been there. And so the writer, now, is doing his best to get them back on track and to speak to the psychological need for encouragement. And what he does, he masterfully presents a powerful case of the superiority of Jesus Christ, and he literally is saying to them, you already have the best. Jesus is better than the angels. He's better than Moses. He's better than Aaron, and He's better than any system you could have been a part of, so why don't you just hold on and believe. You've got to trust, when you can't control. You've got to trust.

"So in chapter 12, he reaches, now, all the way back to every person who had ever walked with God and he said, 'Wherefore seeing we also are compassed about with so great a cloud of witnesses, let us lay aside every weight, and the sin which doth so easily beset us, and let us run with patience the race that is set before us, Looking unto Jesus the author and finisher of our faith; who for the joy that was set before him endured the cross, despising the shame, and is set down at the right hand of the throne of God. For consider him that endured such contradiction of sinners against himself, lest ye be wearied and faint in your minds.' Now, I want you to see—'seeing we are compassed about with so great a cloud of witnesses...' to 'looking unto Jesus.' He is the reason you're expected to win.

"The writer, now, has to make the case of the superiority of Jesus and the superiority of the new covenant and faith which perceiving Him who is invisible. Again, it becomes very basic, in my way of thinking. And that is, we're caught between our perception and what we believe. Oftentimes, when we come to church, church is like a marriage; that is, you get into marriage and you have a concept of what marriage should be like. Everybody here, particularly those of us who have been married and aren't married now, but we've experienced marriage. We're probably a little more realistic, because we understand some things happen in marriage that you never figured or thought about before you got married. And you go to scratching your head about it because you've never been married. And for those of us who have been there and done that, we'll probably be better the second time around, because we won't approach it with some unrealistic concepts.

"Marriage is funny, it's like coming to church; that is, you have a concept in your mind of what your marriage will be, and when you get in it, you find that the person who you married doesn't fit the concept. So right away, you've got what is real and what is perceived, and oftentimes the two don't match. And it becomes extremely difficult sometimes to make an adjustment between what is real and what is perceived.

"And sometimes, perception is as intense and as powerful as reality, and we don't always release our perceptions when we face reality. Sometimes we try to bend reality into becoming what we perceive, only to find out that it is a lesson in futility. Because you cannot take what is real and make it into something that's perceptive; no, no, no, you've got to make that adjustment.

"And it's the same way when you come to church; that is, you have a perception of what this walk with God is going to be and you have a view, and oftentimes the view has been corroborated by the preacher. We've marketed the Lord in a certain way that is very self-serving (I think) and not reality to the people who are coming to God. And what we do is we give them a concept of God that is not always a Biblical concept. It might be my marketing ability to project Him in a way that will get the numbers or that will get the people to come into the house, but the truth is that oftentimes He is projected in a way that is not real. And so, now, it becomes a problem. Why? Because when I came in, I came in with certain expectations.

"I didn't imagine that I wouldn't have all that I wanted. I didn't imagine that my life would still have some struggles and some difficulties and habits that still need changing. I thought that when I got in here that everything would be all right. But I guess they didn't tell me when; they didn't give me a timetable, there was no schedule. But consequently, it leaves me with the struggle now, because I'm dealing with my perception. And I'm dealing with the presentation that I received coming in. I came in because of certain things that I thought would take place. And some have and some have not, yet, taken place.

Redoing My Expectations

"But it's between the time of my receiving God and the time of my consummation of my salvation that I'm having the difficulty, it's between. Because now, He is trying to redo my concepts, but my original concepts have met great disappointment because this is what I thought. I can see you having this discussion with God; I thought this is what was meant by that. Many times, you have discussions with people, and you say I thought this is what it was supposed to be. But you misunderstood me is the response. But I thought! So now I've got to get over the disappointment of having had a certain expectation. And now you're redoing my expectation to give me a reality check, so that now I can go about it the right way. But I don't just make the switch; even though I was wrong, my expectation was deeply imbedded in my spirit and in my attitude. And so the writer now has to bring us to the place where we can understand faith and trusting God and having a relationship with God that completely shatters and changes our expectation. Shattered expectation can break an individual into. Because I'm upbeat by what I expect and when my upbeat, vivacious attitude is completely shattered by the lack of fulfillment of my expectation, it will almost make me walk away, unless somebody can quickly infuse in my spirit what God actually intended in the first place.

"I'm not coming as quickly as you thought; there is some work I have to do on you. I'm not coming as quickly as you thought, because there are other people that I have to reach. I just want you to enjoy Me, if you can't enjoy your circumstances; I want you to enjoy Me, if you can't enjoy your situation; I want you to enjoy Me. I want you to enjoy Me so much that even those who despise you can't shake you because you enjoy Me.

"You see the Hall of Faith-ers then, which was outlined in chapter 11. He lays out a legacy of men and women who have had to endure some things. Many times, we read the Hall of Faith-ers in chapter 11, and if you notice that even in the contemporary, neo-Pentecostal, charismatic environment in which we live, everybody deals with those faith-ers who achieved or received the end of their expectation. But nobody deals with those that are over in, about verse 32 of chapter 11. And I'm just going to read...'And what shall I more say? For the time would fail me to tell of Gideon, and of Barak, and of Sampson, and of Jepthal; of David also, and of Samuel, and of the prophets: Who through faith subdued kingdoms, wrought righteousness, obtained promises, stopped the mouths of lions, Quenched the violence of fire, escaped the edge of the sword, out of weakness were made strong, waxed valiant in fight, turned to flight the armies of the aliens.' This is all faith-ers who have achieved and who have stood up and who have received the end. 'Women received their dead raised to life again: and other...' Uh, oh; uh, oh, now here's a switch now. Because most of us would want to stop at 'women received their dead raised to life; but others were tortured, not accepting deliverance; that they might obtain a better resurrection: And others had trial of cruel mockings and scourgings, yea, moreover of bonds and imprisonment: They were stoned, they were sawn asunder, were tempted, were slain with the sword: they wandered about in sheepskins and goatskins; being destitute, afflicted, tormented.' Now here's what He says...'Of whom the world was not worthy.'

"I wish you could see then, the expectation and the reality. Some people fall within the expectation of the first part of chapter 11, but other people fall into the reality of chapter 11, which is the second part of chapter 11, which means then, that those who have received the end of their expectation and those who had shattered expectation are still one and the same group. In other words, God was not less operating in the life of those who had everything they expected, than any less than in the life of those who had to be sawn asunder or those who were afflicted, destitute and walked around in sheepskin and goatskin. Some were rich and God was with them; some were poor and God was with them; some were delivered and others wouldn't accept deliverance, because the measure of the power of God working in your life has nothing to do with your situation. It has to do with your trust in God to see you through whatever cards you have been dealt.

"You're expected to win! I'm telling you, I don't care what you drove up here in; I don't care what you're wearing; I don't care how far delinquent you are...you're expected to hang in there, until the race is over.

"It is the close, and he closes this chapter now, because the experience is packaged in such a way that the New Testament saint must look at them and understand the power that is in this witness. Here he said in the close: 'And these all, having obtained a good report through faith, received not the promise: God having provided some better thing for us, that they without us should not be made perfect.' What they went through was to give us the evidence that situation does not limit relationship with God, because really, that's why we're here. We have made it quite modern, and of course it has served the church and the preacher quite well, but it has not given the child of God proper expectation as it relates to God. It's easier to market God to you indicating to you if you just believe God, everything in your life is going to be fixed. Don't play with me, please! Don't play with me!

"I can really market the Lord in a manner that you'll get up and run up here and put your money down. And of course, you're putting your money down based on me telling you that now I want you to exercise your faith. Just exercise it and God's going to turn everything around. Yet seven days and everything will be fixed! So now I have given you to expect that based on your participation at the altar, by placing your money, you have just exercised your faith. But please, tell me, can you exercise your faith if you have no money? Can I exercise my faith and not have a dime, or do I have to have some money in order to exercise my faith? Please! Faith is not contained in whether you have money or not. You can be in here just as broke as you can be and still have a relationship with God.

"Don't give up over your finances; don't give up being single all these years. The point is, it's not just your money that makes for your relationship with God. And the exercise of faith is just as powerful when you're walking with God and you're not realizing financial gain. That's when I know you have power with God is when you can have a relationship with God without anything but God. I can praise Him and lift Him up and glorify Him and be positive in my mind that I'm a winner, in spite of my bank account. And so, it is then, that this is the faith that leads to spiritual experiences.

Called to Bear Witness

"So, the wherefore in the text gathers all the heroes of chapter 11 and places them over us as covering. And he places them over us and he says now, 'I want you to look at a plethora of different experiences; I'm not just bringing you one type of experience. I'm bringing you folk who prayed and got healed; folk who prayed and folk were raised from the dead. And I'm bringing you also another group who prayed and still were afflicted and still went to the sword. I'm bringing you a variety, a diversity of people in different ages, from different walks. And I brought them and set them before you as a cloud.'

"What he does now is say, 'I want to put a blanket over you, because you seem to be shivering under the stress of not having realized dreams and not having fulfilled expectation. And I want to cover you, and the blanket that I'm going to use is everybody who preceded you who was in one aspect or another, in relationship with me without the trimmings.'

"Anybody here remember Grandma's quilt, and how she would put together a blanket with different pieces of material? Oh, it looked like a mess, until it was finished! And then it became one of the most beautiful things, because it just wasn't bland, it just wasn't one color but a multiplicity of colors. Well, that's what the Lord did. He moved and He took lives like Gideon and David, and He took lives like Sampson and Barak; He took lives like Rahab and what He did, He put together a blanket, so that when you look at the covering that He's placed on you, you can say to yourself, 'I might not be a David, but I can fit with this Rahab woman. I might not be Rahab, but I can sure identify with Gideon. But at the end of the day, I'm coming out all right.' Because the only reason He gives me the blanket is to tell me that if they had to go through, then surely you've got to get up from where you are, shake off your discouragement, and tell the devil, 'as long as I live, I'm going to be an overcomer.' Oh, you've got some witnesses! You've got some folk watching you! And some folk who have already decided you have to win. Why? Because your winning does something to perfect them; if you don't win, a whole generation, centuries of Christians, of people who followed God would not be made perfect. Because you have the Holy Spirit, you have them for an example, when they didn't have you. You're more equipped than anybody who has ever walked with God. And they're looking at you, cheering you on. Get up, try again! Move again! Pray again! Fast again! Holler again! Read your Bible again! Change your mind, because we're not going to let you die, when it's time for you to live.

"Shake somebody's hand and say, 'Neighbor, you're expected to win.' I know somebody walked out on you, but you're expected to recover. I know somebody thinks you're left for dead, but you're expected to get up. Shake it off and let them know it ain't over yet. I'm still a child of God.

"So the word witnesses becomes significant to the text, because it comes from a Greek word, martus. And martus here is one who testifies or one who can testify. And the only thing that qualifies for testimony is what he has seen or heard or knows by means. It becomes a legal term, witnesses to a contract for a legal document. And what he says is, now we have somebody signing or designated to sign. Oh, God! From somebody who has proved the strength and genuineness of their faith in the Lord

Jesus Christ by undergoing violent death; those who would hold on until death comes, because I've come this way to stay, until I die. And death then brings the potential for resurrection. So I'm moving in this thing with everything I have, and I have witnesses who can declare that they have seen the power of God. Every now and then, I need confirmation because when my sight isn't working, 'faith cometh by hearing, and hearing by the word of God.' And this is why you have to understand the difference between the word of the preacher and the word of God, because they are not always one and the same. Oh, I feel the truth moving in this house!

"You've got to grasp the significance, because you're going to have to hold onto the word of God when the preacher's not around, when your prayer partner has backslidden. You're going to have to hold onto the word of God, because they represent the power that moves you into faith. When your faith is getting weak, you need a confirmation. I need to hear what David said; I need to hear what Paul said. I need to understand is there anybody in this reference, in this quilt that is over me, who has experienced what I'm going through? How did they come out? How did they survive? That same God that was with them, that same God is with me. That's why contemporary saints ought to talk to each other. You ought to talk to your brothers and sisters, and quit trying to hide your embarrassments because God turns embarrassments into testimonies. And when you get over a thing, you don't have to hide it and try to cover it. I was there, now I'm here. Embarrassments have to be turned to testimonies, and you're trying to hide from your daughter your past; you're trying to hide from your son your past. You're trying to cover up the foolish things that you have done that God, miraculously, brought you out of. But the truth of the matter is that somebody very close to you needs to understand that you were not always that Miss-goodie-two-shoes or that Mister right now! But God brought you through. Can I get a witness? Yeah, I can get a witness.

"And so now it's the redeemed of the Lord who ought to say so! Called to bear witness because the church needs to bear witness! And now they are spectators in the stand, not just looking, they're testifying as an example of faith. Not only to look at them but to believe more fully on Christ through them; if they could get through it, I can get through it. And all spiritual men and women, then, have had to live by faith. 'The just shall live by faith.' It's not by what you see, but it's by what you believe. Because it's my faith that controls and moves my will, I don't will to believe; I believe to will, because will is not central; that's another whole conversation. Will is not central, will is influenced. I either will allow my will to be influenced by my situation or my will to be influenced by my faith. If I let my situation influence my will, it will soon become a won't, but if I let my faith influence my will, I will look at every circumstance and declare, at the end of the day, 'I will win.' Because I'm expected by the Holy Ghost, the Word of God and the witnesses to get up out of this condition and tell the devil, 'I'm gone. Break my plate! I'm out of here!'

The Intense, Unending Race

"It is here, then, that the intense, unending race becomes the problem. The hard part is what faith motivates in the arena, spiritual versus carnal or material or earthly. And that's now why he says, you've got to lay aside every weight. And weight now becomes bulk or mass; it's a swelling of superfluous flesh, really, from the Greek. And what he's saying is you've got to lay aside some stuff, because the more you're trying to carry with you, the slower you're going to go and the more tired you're going to become. You need to sit down and put a list out of the stuff you are battling with, that you need to cut loose. Oh, it's some stuff clogging up your life; it's some stuff messing with your life; it's some people that's just sitting there like clogs, clogging up the drain, clogging up your attitude, clogging up your disposition. You thought about some of them this week. But it's some folk you need to let go. I'm sorry, but you just need to let them go. And I'm not talking about not being around them; I'm talking about letting them go, up in your mind. Amen! It's some folk that you're looking for validation from, that aren't in the quilt. God says, I got some folk you need to look at, if you're trying to go somewhere with your life.

"But it looks like the devil's got him a quilt, too, that he's trying to cover me with this negative quilt. But devil, you're too late. God has already put some folk in my life that know how to move from one place to another. And I'm getting ready to shake off some of this extra fat, some of this stuff that's clogging my arteries, trying to stop my heart from flowing. There's folk that will discourage you and break you down and cause you to feel like you're not a winner and talk a lot of negative junk to you and got all kinds of classifications for you. And you sit around hoping they'll validate you; they're not supposed to. They don't have a testimony; they haven't been brought out of nothing; they haven't overcome anything. How do they qualify to sign your document? The devil is a liar! What qualifies you to sign my document? What have you seen? What have you been through? What have you overcome? What have you had to fight out of? What have you had to beg God to bring you out of? I need somebody on the paper who's got a name that God has been with them.

"The allusion here is to a preparatory period where superfluous flesh is rid before the race. He's got to rid himself of some stuff that looks good on the surface, it looks innocent, but indeed and in fact, it clogs him on the inside. Ah, that's all right, it ain't nothing to it. Watching TV eight hours a day—it looks innocent on the outside, but what could you do that's positive with that time, than sitting down looking at the hell-a-vision for eight hours, when God has a book in your spirit, when God has a word in your heart, when God has a purpose for you. And Satan's got you married to a TV, when you ought to be doing something for the community. I wish I could talk to you. Oh, sitting around. It's innocent to go fall in love; it's good, but when you've got purpose and you've got something to do with your life, you've got to do more than just sit around trying to be in love with somebody. I ain't running after love, let love catch up with me!

"It's by running now; it's by running that the saint learns what these things are. So long as he stands still, he does not feel they are burdensome. But when he begins to move in the race, and as he begins to find the hills to climb, now he understands that some things are hindering me. Folk who are standing still going nowhere, well, they don't feel anything, because they aren't carrying any weight.

"I learned some things swimming. If you're swimming, as an exercise, what the body does is it gives you some insulation; because the water, generally, is colder than the body, so there's a thin layer of fat that the body provides when you do a lot of swimming. When you ride a bike, the body doesn't shed weight as quickly, because you're sitting there pedaling and the intensity of the heat in the body that burns fat is not there. But when you're running, it's the greatest core of heat because what the body says is, 'I need to get lighter because I'm carrying this weight around.' It is in running this race, not swimming it; it is in running this race, not being in a car, but being on foot that you begin to understand 'I don't need this person here. And this person ain't the right one for me.' Nah! That ain't the man that fits God's purpose and that sure ain't the woman, because I'm running this race and I'm feeling some weight. That ain't the right leader for me; that ain't what I need to involve myself in right there, because I'm running this race, and I'm feeling some weight. When I should be getting some encouragement, that ain't the right church for me; it's too depressing, because I'm running a race and every day I've got to get to the place where I know I've got the power to win. And so now I've got to decide to get close to Jesus, because now that I'm running, I've got to decide to develop my gift; because now that I'm running, I'm calling and drawing on everything that is in me to get to where God wants me to go.

"The weight here has the idea of an encumbrance. You think you have a lot together before the race, but when you get in the race you find out, 'I've got to look to Jesus. I can't let Him out of my sight.' And then, of course, the race becomes the specific problem because now in the race, I find I've got some stuff that so easily besets me. It's because I'm moving in God that things are being exposed. If I were not moving in God, I could settle for anything and everything. But when I'm moving towards the prize, the mark of the prize of the high calling, now I'm discovering certain things about myself that I would not have discovered if I was standing still.

"That's why some folk don't have time to gossip, because I've got a life and I'm living my life. And I've found that I don't need to put my life on hold, to talk about somebody else's life. I've got something to do with myself. I've got my family unit; I've got to raise my children; I've got to outline their future. So I don't have time to spend with folk, lollygagging over at the restaurant, when I've got to move on. I don't have time to talk about what somebody successful is doing, when I'm trying to move into success myself. I've got something to do, excuse me! I can't be on this phone for an hour. Are you busy? I'm always busy! Touch your neighbor, and say, 'you're expected to win.'

Hold Out to the Finish

"Then you find out you are your own problem. You allow people and things around you to burden you down. The thing you have a proclivity for that is weak in you, that you bring other things around you, because of a tendency that you have. But the race will cause you to correct all of your weak tendencies. That's why you've got to practice coming out of the blocks. You've got to get your stamina coming around the turn. You've got to know how to hold out to the finish and pace yourself. Because a demanding race brings out weaknesses, like demanding faith walk brings out our deficiencies. And so, the writer says, now that the demanding race has brought unbelief out. You did not know that you didn't have that much faith, until you got in some circumstances that were tough. Now I've found I need some more word because in order for me to make this, I need some more word from the Lord. In order for me to get through this, I need some folk who know how to encourage, because I've got to run this race with patience. I've got to learn how to hupomone (Greek for a remaining under), especially, when there's no relief in sight. I've got to learn, when I come round the stretch and thought I was coming to home base, but when I looked up, I see the road is still going on—I've got to learn how to hang in there. Because my first tendency is I need to quit, because I'm not getting anywhere. But I've come too far, with too many witnesses, with too many testimonies, with too many people who can stand up and declare 'keep on coming, we're still believing God for you.' That's why I've got to have some folk in my life, that God gives discernment, who can just come by, without looking to get in nobody's business, but know how to look at you and say, 'I'm praying for you. I won't take any time to talk to you, but I've been talking to God about you.'

"This hupomone includes its passive endurance, where sometimes you've just got to sit it out. Sit it out, when the rage of the enemy is on you. Sometimes you've just got to lean back and declare, 'this too will pass, if I can just hold out through this, and keep my mind stayed on Him, keep my vision on the Lord through here, this too will go by.' But at the same time, it's active, and this is its persistence, and that is, I don't take no for an answer; when Jesus and I have outlined this vision, Jesus and I will get it done, because I heard Him say 'without me you can do nothing.' So it's a two kind of thing here.

It's a holding out; it's a hanging in, when it looks like there's no relief in sight. But it's a going through and a going over, when the obstacle comes in your face. When I don't see relief, I hang in and I hold out. I praise Him with everything I have. And I lift Him up from my spirit.

"But supreme tests call for supreme encouragement. Who and what to do and who to look at, and He says when you're going through, you've got to look to Jesus. Tell somebody, take your eyes off your trials and put your eyes to Jesus. From the Greek, afero, which means to turn your eyes away from others, fix it on Jesus. Jesus brought me here; Jesus started me up; Jesus is my role and Jesus is my model. I refuse to look at the circumstances, when I can look at the Savior, and lift Him up and give Him the glory because He is my leader. Because Jesus is a winner, went all the way down into hell, death and the grave, but picked the devil's pocket, came back up on resurrection morning and declared, all power is in my hand. It looked like I was losing; it looked like I was through, but I came back with a mighty resurrection.

"Sometimes you've got to go to hell, but there is always a mighty resurrection; cause, 'Yea though I walk through the valley of the shadow of death, I will fear no evil, for thou art with me' (Psalm 23:4a). You need an attitude adjustment, because you are a winner, not a loser. You will overcome; you will not be defeated. This is your race, this is your anointing, this is your victory and this is your time. The devil's trying to tell you it's not your time, but you can tell him for me, I've come through too much for the victory not to be won. I've cried too much to lose this victory, for this is life and death. This is soul and eternity. Some things I can lose, but I can't lose this. I can't lose my soul. I can't lose my purpose. I can't afford to lose my anointing. You're expected to win; you're expected to come out; you're expected to move to the next level.

"But somebody said 'Where is the Lord when I'm going through? Where is the Lord in the middle of my trial? Where is the Lord in the middle of my pain? Where is the Lord when I'm hurting like this?' Can I tell you where He is! He's waiting at the finish line because He knows you're coming through. He's waiting at the victory stand because He knows you're coming. Touch your neighbor and say 'I'm on the way, on the way through.' I might not run as fast as you, but He's waiting. If I'm not crying about you, it's because I expect you to come out of here. I expect you to sign that contract. I expect you to get that education. I expect you to buy that house, get out of that rent district and own something for yourself. I expect you to lift up holy hands and give God the glory, even though the man is gone! Even though the woman left! I expect you to bounce back with more power than you've ever had!

"Win, then, just win! I can hear Him cheering us on...I hear Him cheering us on...Come on! Come on! Come on! Read that Bible! Fast! Come on! Pray! You're expected to win. Noah expects it; Gideon expects it; Sampson expects it; you're covered by a cloud of witnesses."

I Had to Write

That is the reason why I had to write these books, because I have people on the other side waiting and looking for me. God sent His word in such a powerful manner, I had to do something; I could not just sit and hear His word and do nothing. I had to write these books, because my children and grandchildren are looking at me and they are trying to see Christ in me. And I'm pointing them to Jesus every step of the way. I'm telling them that the Lord is faithful; I'm telling them the Lord will make a way; I'm telling them the Lord will bring them out and He will bring them through.

So I'm telling you, I had to write these books because there are some people that need an example of what it means to hold onto the promises of God. They are looking for examples today of what it means to hope in His word. Yes, they hear what we as preachers and teachers say, but they are looking to see if we're going to hold out through our own tests and our own trials. We have to let them know, we're still looking to Jesus along with them, because there are some promises that we are still waiting for too! Luke wrote,

> *And the Lord said, Simon, Simon, behold, Satan hath desired to have you, that he may sift you as wheat: But I have prayed for thee, that thy faith fail not: and when thou art converted, strengthen thy brethren* (St. Luke 22:31-32).

Many people are searching and trying to find their way. They desperately want to believe in the God of the Bible. But they struggle to see the relevance of Old Testament scriptures; they struggle to grasp the truth of the word of God. But let me encourage you not to give up; keep coming His way. Paul encourages us by saying,

> *Being confident of this very thing, that he which hath begun a good work in you will perform it until the day of Jesus Christ* (Philippians 1:6).

My Quilt

Let me share with you just a few persons who make up my quilt. Of course, all of my family members are included in my quilt. However, I have been influenced by so many people, whether from past history or the present. I have learned not only by hearing the word of God, but by observing others. There are many people who I have never met and that I may never meet, but they have touched my life in an irrevocable manner. I have watched countless athletes during the Olympics. Some have stumbled and fallen, but they got back up. I watched some of them limp or crawl across the finish line, because they were determined to cross the line. And Pastor Anderson taught me in order to have a place you have to cross the line. I have seen many great Olympians run the 400 meters. Although they push their bodies to the max. they know how to pace themselves for the long haul. Coming down the stretch they're thinking about position, and many have learned how to remain poised. They have learned how to stay calm and trust in their ability to make it. But in this spiritual race, I had to learn how to stay calm and trust in the Lord, because I knew without Him I would not make it. What I am saying is you have to trust God and what He is doing in your life. You have to stay calm and observe and learn from the instructors He has placed in your life. You have to sharpen your listening skills as well as your observation skills. When doing the will of God, you have to learn how to have poise, which is balance, self-assurance, composure, stability and dignity of manner. He gives you all of those qualities, so you can make the race.

My childhood friend since elementary school, Yvonne, has a patch in my quilt. As children, we used to play baseball in the alley with the utility poles being our bases. I could not hit the ball most of the time, because I was afraid of being hit by the ball being thrown at me. So as the teams were being formed, because my friend was always one of the captains, she would always choose me to be on her team. She would choose me first, so I wouldn't feel bad about being chosen last or not being chosen at all. But when she would choose me, she would always call out "last bat," which meant if I got two strikes, she would step up to the plate and hit the last ball. So all I had to do was run around the bases. Now that was a part of my good old days! And that sounds like Jesus to me in that simple analogy! He knew I was going to strike out, so He called out, "last bat!"

Pastor Clifford Dunlap of Greater Love Tabernacle has a patch in my quilt, not only because he introduced me to the writings of Watchman Nee, which helped me in my spiritual growth, but more importantly because when my children would call me in California stating they were having marital problems, I would tell them to call Pastor Dunlap. Pastor and Mother Dunlap have been married for over fifty or sixty years, and they are still going strong. So who better to tell them how to stay together, and so far the two couples he has counseled are still together. And I appreciate him so much for taking time with my children, more than these few words can express.

And there are many, many mothers in the church that gave me instructions, and I will never forget their teaching: My own grandmother, Mother Adell Anderson, who taught me the importance of praying for my children; the late Mother Victoria Pratt, who taught me to serve my children on my best dishes, so they would have an appreciation of nice things; Mother Rebie Owens, my neighbor of twenty years, who counseled with me over the fence as we tended our gardens; and our church mother at Greater Rose, Mother Dorothy Davis, who taught me how to acknowledge God as my father, just by listening to her pray, when it was really difficult for me to call anyone father; and Sister Barbara Anderson, my pastor's wife, who taught me how to have balance in my life.

I have been blessed to have many genteel, gracious women to touch my life, and I pray that I carry myself in like manner.

And do not think I have neglected my own mother, because Mother Thelma Morris is most definitely woven throughout my quilt. I love and appreciate her more than I can express. She worked hard, sometimes working two and three jobs to provide for me and my sisters, and as a child, I did not lack for anything other than her. But I learned early in my young adult life that I had to depend on God. The Psalmist said,

> *When my father and my mother forsake me, then the* L*ORD* *will take me up* (Psalm 27:10).

So when someone said to me that my mother would never get saved for whatever the reason, the thought hurt and frightened me. We may not have been close, nor did we have the kind of relationship that I wanted, but she is my mother. And I went to the Lord in prayer for her. I prayed and asked Him to save my mother, because I loved her enough to stand in the gap. Someone needs to know this too, because most people think it is always the other way around—parents praying for their children to get saved. But it does not matter who intercedes for who, just as long as somebody is praying. I just thank God for His mercy and His kindness, because she loves the Lord with all of her heart. And as an usher for over fifty years, she serves Him with all her might. And I feel honored and privileged that she respects who He has made me.

He Sent Me to Encourage

Yes, the Lord dug deep into the depth of my spirit to bring up this seed of faith and openness that He had planted in me. And I am thankful; I am grateful that He did not allow the devil to destroy me. He did not allow him to destroy my mind, and He has allowed me this privilege and opportunity to share with you. He kept me alive.

There would have been no new challenges for me if I had stayed in the same church affiliation. He has restored and given me new life for His glory. He sent me out to serve His people. He sent me to encourage somebody to hold on, to keep striving, to keep pressing. There are many of us who did not start out as well as we would have liked, but we have hope. Many of us still do not have the education that we want, but I heard Paul say,

> *Now when they saw the boldness of Peter and John, and perceived that they were unlearned and ignorant men, they marveled; and they took knowledge of them, that they had been with Jesus* (Acts 4:13).

The Lord removes all of our excuses. And you cannot say you cannot make it, because I am proof that you can. Because again he said,

> *But God hath chosen the foolish things of the world to confound the wise; and God hath chosen the weak things of the world to confound the things which are mighty* (1 Corinthians 1:27).

And as long as there is life, there is hope. Be encouraged not to give up on your dreams. Stay in the race, and cross the finish line.

I pray this little book will strengthen and encourage you in the faith. I hope that it will dig deep into the depths of who you are and bring up the hidden treasures God has placed within you too. I pray you will read and re-read the messages that have been included for your edification and that you will value the word of God. I pray it will bring clarity for those who do not easily grasp the reality of our faith, which will cause us to do something.

Thank you, every reader, for the privilege to serve you in my writing, because my ultimate purpose is to hear the Lord say "well done, my good and faithful servant!" And with that I rest my case!

Endnotes

[1] Martin Luther, *Bondage of the Will,* translated by J.I. Packer and O.R. Johnston (Fleming H. Revell, 1957).

[2] Paul Tillich, *Dynamics of Faith* (HarperCollins Publishers Inc., 1957) pp. 1-5, 7-8, 10-11.

[3] Bishop Noel Jones, *Don't Faint*, September 7, 2003, Noel Jones Ministries.

[4] Dr. Martin Luther King, Jr., *A Testament of Hope*, edited by James Melvin Washington (Harper & Row, Publishers, Inc., 1986) pp. 259-267.

[5] Bishop Noel Jones, *You're Expected to Win*, February 27, 2005, Noel Jones Ministries.